New YORK *to* *Buenos* AIRES
IN 16 DAYS

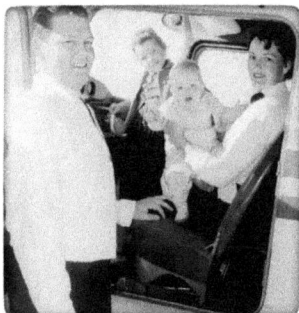

New York *to* *Buenos* AIRES
IN 16 DAYS

ROBERT E. WELLS

Cover design by Ivica Jandrijevic
Map illustrations by Mariya Foteva
Interior layout and design by www.writingnights.org
Book preparation by Chad Robertson
Edited by Elayne Wells Harmer

ISBN: 978-1-7365629-0-1
LIBRARY OF CONGRESS CATALOGING-IN-PUBLICATION DATA:
NAMES: Wells, Robert E., author.
TITLE: New York to Buenos Aires in 16 Days –
The Daring Adventure of a Young Family's Intercontinental Flight in a Single-
Engine Plane/ Robert E. Wells.
DESCRIPTION: Patagonia Press, Salt Lake City, Utah, 2021.
IDENTIFIERS: ISBN 9781736562901 (Perfect bound) |
SUBJECTS: | Memoir | Aviation | Travel | Adventure |
CLASSIFICATION: Pending
LC record pending

Patagonia Press
Printed in the United States of America
Printed on acid-free paper

This book is a memoir.

24   23   22   21   20   8   7   6   5   4   3   2   1

To Meryl, Susan, and Bob,
for being the wind beneath my wings

To Helen,
for her love and support for fifty-eight years

CONTENTS

Las Vegas

New York

Mazatlán
Guadalajara
Acapulco
San Salvador

Panama
City

Medellín
Cali

Guayaquil

Lima

Aconcagua
Mendoza
Santiago

Buenos Aires

Chapter One

LAS VEGAS → NEW YORK
IN THREE DAYS

THE STORY OF my great intercontinental adventure in 1956 began several years earlier, when my wife and I were living in Buenos Aires, Argentina. Meryl had just received her private pilot's license after flying a Piper Cub at the San Fernando grass-field airport and club.

The U.S. Navy had trained me as a pilot from early 1945 to late 1947 under the Holloway Plan. Named for Adm. James Holloway, the program provided free training in exchange for a four-year commitment in the regular Navy as a midshipman/aviation cadet.

In late 1947, the Navy wanted to cancel that program, but they gave us cadets a choice: We could stay in the Navy, or we could receive an honorable discharge along with the GI Bill for two and a half years at any university. The problem with option one was that the Navy did not need more pilots or officers since the war was over, so I left the Navy to earn my bachelor's degree. I studied petroleum engineering at Cal Berkeley but graduated from Brigham Young University in accounting and economics (what I like to call "the science of money"). After I submitted my missionary papers, the Church* assigned me to Argentina, where I served from September 1949 to April 1952.

While working as the finance secretary at mission headquarters, I met Jack Arnold, executive director of Citibank in Buenos Aires. After I caught Citibank in an accounting error, Mr. Arnold offered me a job in international banking on the spot, effective at the end of the mission. I returned home to Las Vegas, Nevada, and within two months married Meryl Leavitt, who had waited for me during my mission. One month later, I started work in New York City on Wall Street at the headquarters of The National City Bank of New York (NCB).*

After two months of training at 55 Wall Street headquarters, instead of the usual two years, I was assigned to Argentina, where I was trained in the operations department. That was unusual, because most trainees were assigned to the credit department. In my spare time, I rented small fabric-covered Pipers and Stinsons to build flying hours and experience; I also bought a half-interest in a classic thirty-foot sailboat. Meryl

---

* The Church of Jesus Christ of Latter-day Saints.
* After several iterations since its founding in 1812 as City Bank of New York, the bank was formally renamed "Citibank" in 1976.

happily joined me in both hobbies. I taught her to fly, and soon she was ready to get her license.

The Argentine government flight inspector assigned for Meryl's checkride decided to check her vision by flying low over a railroad station. He asked her to read the name for him. She looked at it and shook her head, so he thought she had some kind of sight impairment and returned immediately to the club hangar, where I was waiting.

"Your wife is blind. She can't see!" he said.

I asked my upset wife what had happened.

She answered indignantly, "He asked me to read that long train station sign! I could see it okay, but I had no idea how to pronounce the darn name."

I asked him the name of the train station.

"Ingeniero Jacobacci," he responded.

She had acquired some basic Spanish for social conversations, but no way could she pronounce all eight syllables in Spanish of the two-word station name! They went back up and she passed the flying part of her final private license test with flying colors.

In March 1953, a sweet baby girl joined our family. We named her Susan. In November 1955, we were blessed with a little boy whom we named Robert, after my father and me. We called him "Bobby."

At the end of three years' service in Argentina and Brazil, the bank gave us a three-month vacation plus travel time by cruise ship to and from New York, plus any time spent in the 55 Wall Street Head Office for additional training and building social connections with senior officers. We went out West to our home in Las Vegas, and with time on my hands and money in my pocket (a salary advance for about five months), I began looking at small airplanes for sale.

The Cessna dealer in Las Vegas, George Crockett, was kind and knew my family. He asked if I would like to work as a temporary sales rep for him during our vacation, demonstrating new and used airplanes on a commission basis. I did that a few hours each day for fun, and one day George asked me to go to the Cessna factory in Wichita to pick up a new airplane. That was a great and unique new adventure, and led to a wild idea:

Let's fly this to Argentina!

Meryl liked the idea as much as I did. At first, we looked at new planes and their prices, and then we started looking at used planes with much lower prices. I had fallen in love many years before with the famous Staggerwing Beech, a five-person military surplus plane used by the Navy for executives' transportation. It had a big radial engine of 450 hp, constant speed prop, retractable landing gear, and a cruising speed of 200 mph. I had fifty-four hours of Navy time in the Stearman biplanes, eighty-two total hours in the fabulous SNJ (Air Force AT 6), plus another 279 hours logged in various small civilian planes.

The Staggerwing biplane was intimidating to my wife, whose total flying hours were in simple Piper Cubs of the San Fernando Club in Buenos Aires. Plus, I knew that all fabric-covered planes had maintenance problems and that big radial engines of Navy surplus origin needed trained mechanics.

So we downgraded our thinking to the brand-new Cessna 170 line of all-aluminum cabin planes with medium-sized, horizontal, six-cylinder engines. It was a very simple airplane and sat just four people. This was 1956, and Cessna had just come out with the 172, a tricycle-gear model. I picked up the first one at the factory for George, the Cessna dealer, and he offered me a big discount if we wanted to buy it. We weren't sure, so we looked at the North American Navion and the V-tail Beechcraft airplanes. They were much more expensive than the Cessna line, but also faster and fancier. The Pipers of the time were still fabric-covered and cheaper, but the cabin was smaller and not as nice as the all-aluminum Cessna 170 and 172 models.

About this time, my bosses on Wall Street phoned to insist that we spend some time in New York. It would be "good for my career." In other words, they wanted me to socialize with the top brass. I was to bring my lovely, attractive, very intelligent wife (a former department head for Bank of America in Los Angeles) so other people could meet her. We decided it would be a good time to buy one of the planes we were considering, fly it to New York to show it off, and then ask my bosses about letting us fly the plane back down to South America. I knew there was a strong likelihood they would turn down the idea if the trip was risky, but if we flew the plane from Las Vegas to New York in the winter, I figured they would be impressed and find it hard to refuse.

While we were thinking about flying back to Argentina, George took in a used 1949 Cessna 170A. Just a few years old, it was a modern, all-aluminum, four-seat, high-wing, all-purpose airplane. He offered it to me at the ridiculously low price of four thousand dollars, which was extremely generous of him. At that price, I could fly it to New York, and if they turned me down, I could resell it and make a profit. So we bought the little Cessna and both fell in love with it.

However, we weren't entirely prepared for the crazy weather during the cross-country flight from Las Vegas to New York.

We were both born in Las Vegas, and our parents and many relatives lived there. Winter weather is great for flying the western desert, so we took the Cessna out for a test flight from Las Vegas to Los Angeles to visit relatives. We needed to get a feeling for the care and feeding of the plane (gas, oil, tire pressure, etc.), and we also needed to see if we could do three- and four-hour trips with the kids before needing to land for food or bathroom stops. We took a few other trips to visit friends and relatives in Salt Lake City, and flew over Zion Canyon and the Grand Canyon. Flying the plane was as simple as driving any Ford Model A car. Absolutely no problems, and the weather was clear and beautiful. But the trip to the East Coast and back to Las Vegas was a totally different challenge.

Massive winter storms were moving fast from west to east over the country. My Navy meteorology training taught me how to handle the weather, but VFR (Visual Flight Rules) flying in bad weather is tricky. We had no gyro instruments for instrument flying except for one Venturi-driven turn-and-bank. In the Navy, I trained in planes with full-panel gyros and ADF (Automatic Direction Finder) radios. Our 1949 Cessna had nothing but one low-frequency radio for short-distance tower communications (one transmitter frequency only and a receiver that picked up strong commercial radio stations and radio range transmissions with a fixed loop) and one VHF transceiver with five frequencies, but it was also limited to very short line-of-sight range.

We bought maps for the route to New York and made a plan. We would stay behind a strong front that was moving from west to east, fly until we caught up with it, then land and wait till we had better visibility. After leaving Susan and Bobby with Meryl's parents, we flew out of Las Vegas early in the morning and caught up with the winter storm in Wichita, Kansas, where our Cessna was born. We stayed there overnight.

The next morning, we flew until we ran into the back side of the snowstorm, which had moved to Columbus, Ohio. We landed at a small airport outside the city and spent the night. The next morning, the forecasts said the front would move east to New York, but the visibility behind it was lousy. We made a couple of stops, waiting for better visibility.

We cruised at economy power settings to find our best range for longer legs between refueling stops. At 100 mph, the Cessna would burn six gallons of fuel per hour. Luckily we had a tailwind of 20 mph, so we were moving quite rapidly. But approaching New York, I had to go lower and lower to see below me. The haze was so bad, I got some highways mixed up, but I kept moving east. I thought I saw the Hudson River and turned to follow it, but I couldn't tell if I had to turn right or left to find the Teterboro Airport in New Jersey, where I was going to park the plane for the week.

I called the tower on radio frequency 3023.5 and explained my plight. He asked me to describe what I could see below me on the big river. When I did, he said, "I know exactly where you are. Make an immediate right turn, take this compass heading, and you should be over us in about five minutes."

I did what he said, and then out my left side saw the towers of the George Washington Bridge right ahead where I had just been. I was low enough that had I continued, I might have been too low to clear the bridge pylon towers. I found the airport and we tied down outside because the hangars were full. We were safe and sound after flying almost 1,800 miles in three days.

We spent a week in New York socializing with the top brass at Citibank. Toward the end of the week, after Meryl had charmed everyone, I approached my boss.

"Say, Meryl and I have bought a nice single-engine Cessna airplane, and we'd like to fly it back to Argentina," I said casually. "We're both pilots, so it'll be a fun trip. And a plane would be really useful in South America—roads down there are sometimes pretty bad, so this way I could fly to the interior of Argentina and neighboring countries."

My boss was frowning but didn't say anything, so I plowed ahead, making my case.

"Aviation gas is subsidized down there," I explained. "I'd like to ask the bank to give me what it would cost to get my family back to Buenos Aires on a cruise ship, and we'll use the money to fly down instead."

My boss shook his head.

"Nope," he said firmly. "The bank won't approve it."

I was persistent enough that he agreed I could talk to *his* boss. Same result: a firm, "no." It wasn't safe, he said, especially with two little kids.

Undeterred, I kept going up the chain.

I finally got up to the highest officer of the bank and gave him the same pitch. "Bob," he said, "if you want to talk to the president of the bank, James Stillman Rockefeller himself, go ahead. If he throws you out or fires you, it will be your fault."

I called Mr. Rockefeller's secretary and got an appointment that afternoon.

He listened to me talk about my Navy training, my missionary service in Argentina, and my love of adventure. When I was finished, he said with a smile, "Bob, I think if you wanted to get your family back to Argentina in a rowboat, you could do it. I'll approve the flight."

Citibank had thousands of employees, and the worst thing for a career is to be lost in the middle of a very big herd. But I did not have that problem. My story got around, and I was referred to as "that Mormon who flies airplanes." I think it helped me get promotions and advancements throughout my career at the bank.

Las Vegas

New York

Mazatlán

Guadalajara

Chapter Two

NEW YORK → LAS VEGAS
IN FOUR DAYS

W HEN THE BANK made the final calculations, as authorized by Mr. Rockefeller, they ended up giving me the full amount of the cost for a three-week cruise from New York to Buenos Aires in a first-class two-cabin suite on the Moore-McCormack Line. The bank always did things first class in every way, and they treated the international executives very well. They even rounded the amount up slightly and gave me four thousand dollars to get my family back to Argentina.

They had no way of knowing that was the exact amount I had paid to buy my little Cessna. I calculated that the out-of-pocket cost for gas, oil, fees, tips, meals, hotels, etc., would be about five hundred dollars, because the dollar was highly valued in those days, aviation fuel was subsidized by local governments, and the plane itself was remarkably well designed for efficiency and comfort.

Of course, the downside was that I was running the risk of having an accident or landing in some banana republic in the midst of a revolution and having my airplane taken away by force. That had happened to other pilots over the years; some had even been shot down by terrorists. If I survived any of those risks, it would be my responsibility to get my family to Argentina by bus, train, DC-3, or canoe.

Meryl and I determined that there were no known political or social problems in any of the countries we would be flying over or landing in, and that there were no major weather storms such as hurricanes and cyclones forecast along our route for that time of year. We were excited to get back home and start the adventure!

But while our trip from Las Vegas to New York had been helped along by rather constant tailwinds from 10–20 kn, much of the return flight from New York to Las Vegas was into headwinds of about 10–20 kn, except for one leg of the trip into Amarillo, Texas, where the headwinds were a whopping 40 kn.* The cars and trucks below us on that highway going west traveled faster than we did and passed us up. We cruised at 100 mph, but our ground speed on that leg was a miserable 60 mph.

We landed safely at Amarillo, but the wind was so strong we

---

* Wind is always reported in knots rather than miles per hour (an old sailing tradition). A knot (kn) equals 1.15 miles.

could not turn our light plane off the runway. The gale was causing us to weathervane into the wind, so the tower told us to wait. They sent out a pickup truck with some big men to hold down our wings and walk us off the runway and over to a nearby hangar. It worked. We just sat in our seats with the engine off until the hangar doors rolled shut, and stayed in Amarillo that night.

As we flew home, Meryl and I discussed the logistics of our upcoming intercontinental journey.

We had already done the math to figure out fuel consumption. At 100 mph we could get 16.6 miles per gallon, which is good economy at a no-wind cruising speed. We had two fuel tanks, one in each wing, of twenty gallons each, but what we didn't know was whether that was twenty gallons useable or only eighteen, because sometimes the tank isn't installed right in order to drain the last possible drop down to the engine in level flight. Some things you have to try out to learn—like how much fuel you can safely burn before the engine begins to sputter.

Another calculation we had to make was how long we could handle flying without a "potty stop," because sometimes there is not a convenient fuel stop indicated on the map. We had talked to other pilots who had flown small planes from the States to South America and had taken notes of all their advice. It looked like most of our route had good landing fields no more than three-hour legs (300 mi.) apart. There would be two long legs of five hundred miles. The plane's maximum distance before running out of fuel was six hundred miles with no wind, but sometimes winds turn up unexpectedly, so we set a personal maximum of five hundred miles before refueling.

Meryl and I knew we could handle a long stretch like that, but we had to plan for the children's needs. Susan was three years old and very well-behaved and agreeable. But could she go three or four hours without needing a potty break? Bobby was six months old. What would we do about smelly diapers? I let Meryl figure those details out!

We calculated that if we flew about seven hundred miles every day, we could make the eight thousand miles from Las Vegas to Buenos Aires in fourteen days, plus take two extra days to sightsee and rest, one day in Lima, Peru, and one day in Santiago, Chile. We carefully planned a day-by-day itinerary that started in Las Vegas and went down the west coast of South America. We did not fly south from New York for several reasons.

First, we had left Susie and Bobby in Las Vegas, as we still had more vacation time there.

Second, Meryl and I spoke Spanish and were familiar with the Spanish-speaking countries down the Pacific Coast of Latin America. Neither of us was fluent in Portuguese, the language of Brazil down the Atlantic route.

Third, flying down the western part of Mexico and through the countries of Central America and then down the Pacific Coast to Chile and across the Andes to Argentina was the only route our insurance company approved for us. Flying a plane across the Caribbean to Venezuela, across the three Guyanas, across the bulge of Brazil where the Amazon empties into the Atlantic Ocean at the equator, on down the coast to Uruguay and across the River Plate to Argentina was too dangerous, they said.

Fourth, the Pacific route had many more big cities, hospitals, highways, and refueling airports than the Atlantic route. In fact, the major cities on the Pacific Coast were more highly developed and much more sophisticated than any cities of the

Mountain West and Southwest desert area in 1956. Back then, there were only a few hotels on the Highway 91 strip in the desert outside Las Vegas. Many of our friends had no idea that some cities in South America had subways, electric trains, sophisticated theaters, modern hospitals, and world-famous ballet companies and symphony orchestras.

When we got back to Las Vegas and told our friends and family about the wild adventure we had planned, many of them were quite concerned. Of course, a lot of people in 1956 were completely unaware of the progress the aviation industry had made since the war. There were still some great aircrafts on the market from the fabric-and-bamboo 1930s era, but our Cessna 170 represented the post-WWII aviation industry: a very dependable engine, all aluminum, a four-seat cabin, *and* a heater and radio!

But because many people didn't know about modern planes or South America, we would frequently get this question: "You are going to fly a small plane eight thousand miles, all the way to Argentina, with your babies?!"

"Yes," Meryl and I would answer with a smile. "It's a four-passenger Cessna, not a little Piper Cub. This is a plane to match our historic adventure!"

We showed friends and family a picture of our plane's cabin with a cutaway shot illustrating how the cabin is about the size of a Volkswagen Beetle:

We explained that the two of us would sit in front very comfortably, with Susie behind Meryl and Bobby behind me in a little "crib" with folding legs. (It was what we used instead of infant car seats back then.) One set of legs folded on the seat under the crib, and the other set of legs stayed down on the floor behind my seat.

"We have an electric plug for a bottle warmer for Bobby, just like in a car," we explained. "We'll have powdered milk, puréed baby foods, drinks and snacks, and we can buy more when we stop."

Sometimes people asked specific questions about the engine that would fly us that far with no maintenance and no need for special tools. The Cessna did not have a huge radial engine like those in WWII aircraft. We gave them a detailed answer:

"Our plane has a Continental engine, six air-cooled, horizontal-opposed cylinders, 145 hp, and twin sparkplug ignition to every cylinder, but without complicated turbo super-charging for high altitude, no oxygen system to recharge, and no pressurized cabin to fail. It is as dependable as the radial engine that Charles

Lindbergh used to cross the Atlantic nonstop."

Of course, everyone had heard of the fearsome crossing of Aconcagua, the highest mountain in all of North and South America, and many were quite concerned.

"Yes, we're going to cross the Andes, but we will wait for the right weather before we do," we reassured them. "Aconcagua is 22,800 feet at the summit, but the pass is just 12,000. We've both climbed Mt. Timpanogos near Provo, Utah, which is also 12,000 feet. A nonsmoker in normal health can handle that. Our plane can climb up to 15,000 feet, and we can also handle that altitude if the rising air current takes us on up, because we will just be sitting there, exerting no energy, and not needing any extra oxygen. We plan on crossing just above the statue of Christ called 'Cristo de los Andes.' The climb up to the pass takes only a few short minutes to reach the 12,000-foot altitude, and then we drop down steadily, so we are back at 10,000 feet in a few minutes. We won't need oxygen tanks."

Some were still not reassured and thought we were doing something crazy.

But then we'd compare our Cessna 170 with the Ryan Aeronautical airplane made to Charles Lindbergh's specifications in San Diego. In 1927, Lindbergh flew from New York to Paris, three thousand miles nonstop across the Atlantic Ocean, in thirty hours. It was a fabulous and most courageous and historic feat. The Cessna 170 and the *Spirit of St. Louis* are similar in appearance: each is a high-wing monoplane, they are almost exactly the same size, and they fly at about the same air speed:

	Ryan	Cessna 170A
Normal cruise speed	110 mph	110/120 mph
Wingspan	36 ft	36 ft
Nose to tail	27 ft	24 ft
Horsepower	220	145

However, the planes are also very different. One of the biggest differences was the number and capacity of fuel tanks. To fly nonstop for thirty hours, Lindbergh needed four hundred and fifty gallons of fuel on board. It was very tricky to manage the weight and balance of so much fuel. The Cessna 170 had two wing tanks of exactly twenty gallons each with simple gravity feed. Lindbergh, however, placed his main tank right at the center of gravity where the pilot sits. He had to place his own seat toward the tail behind the big cabin tank, so he had no forward vision and no windshield, just two side windows and a small mirror periscope to see directly ahead.

Another big difference is that the Ryan had a classic, hollow steel-tube frame with a fabric cover that was shrunk in place with dope, kind of like shrink wrap. The Cessna 170 had an advanced aluminum cover riveted in place over aluminum forms that gave strength to the wings and fuselage. The Ryan was a bare-bones aircraft with only the essentials; it had no upholstery, heater, or cabin, and just one seat. The comfortable Cessna had nice upholstery, a heater, windows, and a four-seat cabin. Lindbergh flew over mostly open ocean for thirty hours. We would be flying over land the whole way, and we could stop anytime we wanted to refuel the plane, use the restroom, or let Susie run around. We could stay overnight wherever we wanted.

By the time we left Las Vegas, I believe we had persuaded everyone that we would be just fine.

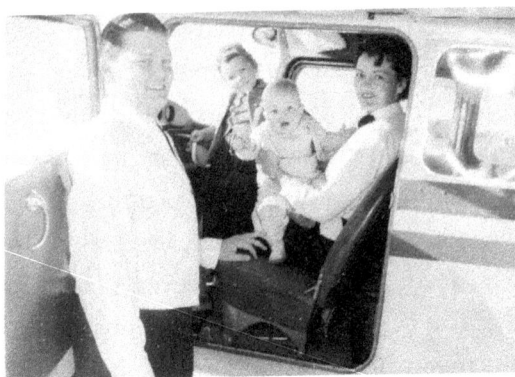

The Wells Family is the pilot, three-year-old Susan, six-month old Bobby and co-pilot Meryl, who learned to fly in Buenos Aires.

Las Vegas

Guaymas

Guadalajara

Acapulco

San Salvador

Managua

San José

Chapter Three

DAY 1

LAS VEGAS → GUAYMAS, MEXICO

DAY 2

GUAYMAS → ACAPULCO

WE LOADED OUR plane and climbed aboard, waving to family and friends who were at the Las Vegas Cessna dealer to see us off to Argentina, about eight thousand miles away. George Crockett, now a good friend, had named his fixed-base operation "Crockett's Alamo." I had spent a few hours each day demonstrating new and used planes for him, and so far, my only sale was a secondhand Cessna 170A to my wife and me.

Our flight plan was intentionally very simple and uncomplicated because we had no idea how long it would take us to get across the border and into Mexico. We both spoke Spanish, we were both licensed pilots, and we had spent the last three years in Argentina and Brazil working for Citibank, but still, you never know if officials will be pleasant or mean.

We had a full set of sectional maps for the trip and had talked to a couple of professional ferry pilots who had flown single-engine planes not equipped for instrument flight from the U.S. to Argentina.

Their advice was fairly simple:

"Follow the coast down to Panama; fly inland to Medellín, Colombia; fly the valley to Cali, Colombia; next fly directly to Guayaquil, Ecuador; then follow the Pacific Coast to Santiago, Chile; cross the Andes at Santiago, Chile; enter Argentina at Mendoza; fly across Argentina to Buenos Aires. Don't mess with the weather—stay on the ground if it's bad. Reports on weather are unreliable and it will likely change suddenly anyway. If you run into any weather, land and wait it out. Be sure you send a telegram to the director of civil aviation of every country you will fly over, advising your approximate date of entering their air space, asking for permission to do so, and keep a copy. It will help, but you will still have to pay some bribes for real or invented failure to comply with that rule or any of their other many rules, so take a wad of small dollar bills. The dollar goes a long way and every official is way underpaid."

Our first stop was in Nogales, Arizona, so we could leave the country properly. The paperwork was tedious. They had never seen a small plane with two crew, a toddler, and a baby with a destination of Argentina. Usually, they saw small planes going to Mexico for fishing or to stay at the famous resort of Acapulco. They had forms with places for "pilot and co-pilot," but seeing little children as passengers was new to them. We still had to make out a passenger manifest with several copies to please them and they insisted that we return the plane to the U.S. eventually, because we did not have papers to export the plane.

The officials said it would be best to cross the border and land in Nogales, Mexico. That turned out to be unnecessary, but we were at their airport, so we had to fill out all the papers again. They had us go through each office and fill out forms for flight plan, immigration, customs, weight and balance, radio license, etc. In the process, the customs inspector discovered the three guns I was carrying: a .38 revolver, a 12-gauge shotgun, and a single-shot .410 pistol. They were all disassembled and stored separately, but I had to show my permit to carry weapons from the Las Vegas sheriff's department.

Some years before, I had joined the sheriff's "Flying Posse" to help search for people lost in the desert or to look for escaped prisoners or just to be useful in any situation. Consequently, I had been sworn in as a deputy sheriff. As I pulled out my wallet, I accidently dropped my Clark County Deputy Sheriff badge and it fell on the floor with a noisy clatter. The official gold-colored multi-pointed badge got everyone's attention. In Spanish, "deputy" can be translated as "diputado," which means a high government official.

The inspector, his eyes wide, asked, "Qué es esto?"

"Soy un sheriff diputado," I answered.

"Como John Wayne??" he exclaimed in awe.

"Sí, Señor. Como John Wayne."

He lit up like it was a great honor to welcome us into his country, and to my great relief he said, "Colega. Pase Usted. No hace falta más tramites. Que tenga un buen viaje." ("Colleague.

Come right in. You do not need any more approvals. Have a good trip.")

No more delays! We were ushered back to our plane, and there were big smiles all around as we waved goodbye. Susie blew kisses and Bobby gurgled happily. From then on, that gold sheriff's badge was on top of our passports and other credentials, and it worked in every country except Nicaragua. The Latin officials are very respectful of military authority of any kind and they all love Western movies and know John Wayne. It may have helped that I wore at all times my Western boots, pants, shirt, bolo tie, and my tooled belt with a big silver belt buckle.

We had lost a lot of time leaving the U.S. and entering Mexico. We only made it down to the coastal port of Guaymas before we had to land. Regulations at that time limited night flying to multi-engine airplanes; single-engine planes had to be on the ground before sundown. Guaymas turned out to be a delightful place with excellent seafood and a very nice hotel. We spent a pleasant night and were up early for a long day of flying because we wanted to get on down the coast to famous Acapulco. The kids ended up traveling very well. The noise in flight of the rushing air and the pulling prop and the exhaust of the engine seemed to lull them to sleep most of the time.

We had scheduled fuel and bathroom stops at Mazatlán, Guadalajara, and a last leg to spend the night at Acapulco. We made the two stops flying down the coast and were treated very cordially. We did have one unexpected problem, though, that illustrates the relaxed environment that existed back in those days. The tower frequency throughout both American continents was the same: 3023.5. We called about fifteen minutes out and no response. Five minutes out and no response. We landed and taxied to the gas truck, which was alongside the tower, a two-story adobe tower with a glass-enclosed space on top for the radio operator. The stairway up was rather rickety and around the outside. The temperature was very warm on the ground and the glassed-in tower must have been twenty degrees hotter.

Another plane called in for landing permission. We could hear someone on the loudspeaker, but there was no one up in the tower to answer. I asked the gas truck man where the tower man was. He pointed to the fellow in the shade, relaxed in a lawn chair. He was not about to climb up into the hot tower. The other plane landed, still calling for permission. When we finished filling our tanks and were ready to leave, I asked the man in the lawn chair why he didn't answer our calls.

"Were you in trouble?" he said, pushing the brim of his hat up to look at me.

"Well, no."

"Was there another plane landing when you called in?"

"No…"

"So why should I climb back up into that hot tower?"

I didn't have a response to that!

Mazatlán

Guadalajara

Acapulco

San Salvador

Chapter Four

DAY 3

ACAPULCO → SAN SALVADOR

ACAPULCO, MEXICO, is a much-storied vacation spot for Hollywood actors and wealthy tourists. It has been featured in magazine articles, gossip columns of the rich and famous, a few movies, and as a watering spot for playboys and politicians. It was once the major Mexican harbor for imports from the Far East and the whole Pacific Rim from Japan and China down to the Philippines.

We flew over the city and the bay and landed at the Acapulco airport. After tying down the plane, we took a taxi into town.

The taxi driver knew where to take us: a prestigious hotel right on the beach. Our suite was very reasonable in price and faced the whole gorgeous harbor lined with tall hotels. He pointed out restaurants within walking distance of our hotel, and also recommended the one in our hotel. He offered to take us to see the local cliff-divers who demonstrated their death-defying acrobatic skills for the amazed tourists. They had to time their dives to match the biggest waves, which caused the safest depths in the churning ocean waves and rocks far below. We drove by the yacht club and the deep-sea fishing boats, whose captains assured us we could catch enormous marlins and sailfish if we rented their services.

Our taxi driver did a great job, but he failed to warn us of one thing: The mariachi bands were great, but very noisy until about two o'clock in the morning. We could hear our hotel band above everything else, but when they took a break, we could hear other bands off in the distance. We did enjoy this famous resort, but thankfully it was only for one night.

The next day, our first leg was down the coast to the Isthmus of Tehuantepec. We took a rest stop, refueled, and flew on down to Tapachula, the required exit airport from Mexico. The sheriff's badge helped us through the complex procedures, but they still took a long time. Having been delayed more than we expected, Meryl and I discussed how to make up the lost time. We knew that if we skipped landing in Guatemala, the adjacent country, we would be ahead of our self-imposed schedule. We also calculated in our minds that every hour spent on the ground going through immigration, customs, fueling, filling out the mandatory flight plan, making out the passenger manifest in quadruplicate, etc., would cost us a hundred miles on the southbound destination for the day.

We had to land before sunset by law, but we figured we still had three or four hours. We would fly down the Guatemalan coast for two hundred miles (two hours at our slow, economy cruise speed), then go inland to find a nice hotel. Unfortunately, I fell into the same trap that had snagged other pilots.

We cruised down the beautiful and interesting tropical coastline of Guatemala without landing. About the time we flew into El Salvador, several things went wrong. The sky, which had been clear, suddenly became cloudy. It was a low and solid bank of stratus clouds. No rain or wind, but solid and low clouds. It was easy to fly under the layer of unexpected clouds at about 1,500 feet above the beach, but to our left was a low, coastal range of hills, and to our right, the pass inside to the San Salvador airport was blocked by low clouds. Our planned entry was impossible.

All of a sudden, it seemed that the cloud layer unexpectedly blocked the last of the sunlight. It was getting dark. It was not supposed to get dark yet! I looked at my watch. We still had two hours of daylight, I thought. Then it hit me like a ton of bricks—I had miscalculated. My watch was still on Las Vegas time! We had flown eastward so far that we had gone two time zones over, making sunset two hours earlier than I had planned. (San Salvador is directly south of New Orleans.)

Night was falling, and the cars on the coastal highway had their lights on. I had to land very soon and there was no airport anywhere. I had to drop the plane onto a safe beach or onto a safe road RIGHT NOW! Either way was a sure accident—which we could survive—but only by sacrificing our plane. I thought I had enough dim visibility to see the white tops of the waves curling up on the beach but feared we would either flip over in beach sand or choose a field with unseen ditches or fences.

Our silent prayers helped. At that moment, underneath us, I spotted an old yellow Stearman biplane parked beside a very large ranch house and corrals. It had to be a crop duster. We had flown over some large fields that looked like banana plantations and they used crop dusters. The big yellow biplane was easier to see, and it was parked in a very small pasture beside a big house. It looked like there were fifty-gallon drums of chemicals and hopefully aviation gas beside the plane, so it had to be a crop duster.

I figured that if he could dump that big biplane into that small field, then I could do the same thing. My Navy flying came in handy, because from the very beginning of training we practiced landings by aiming at the close end of a very short runway, as though it were a small aircraft carrier. We did not fly a long, straight descent but rather came around out of a tight turn, keeping constant sight of the near end of the imaginary carrier.

I slowed down to almost stalling speed, flaps full down, tight turn to the left, keeping the slightly visible darker fence line in sight, turning constantly, keeping the plane on the verge of a stall, even a little below the stall by hanging on the prop, so that the very moment I cleared the near end of the fence I could cut the power and drop hard in a full-fledged three-point stall, dump the flaps, and hit the brakes. We skidded on the pasture a bit but did not nose over and came to a full stop a few feet short of the Stearman, sitting dimly in the dark. If it had not been for the old yellow Navy fabric, I might never have seen it in that field when I was right over it, and I would have had trouble lining up with it at the far end of that dark pasture. We had angels watching over us.

The foreman of the ranch and his family and workers came

out to see who and what had arrived so late in the dark. The Stearman pilot was with them. I thanked him for being parked by the big ranch house so I could see him, and asked, "How in the world did you get into this tiny field? I just barely made it."

He laughed and pointed. "Over there the fence is fixed so I can let down the wires and taxi over them into the much bigger field. I take off and land over there, not here by the house. We'll show you in tomorrow's light. You'll be able to get out when you want to. But you sure did a good job of coming in low and slow and nailing your landing so your rollout was short!"

I accepted the compliment but silently thanked the Lord and those unseen angels for seeing the crop duster plane on the ground and being able to squeeze into the tiny field alongside the big one.

The foreman explained that the ranch owner was a banker in the capital city, and he and his family only came to the ranch on weekends. I gave him my business card. The foreman was impressed with the name of Citibank and my bank title of "pro-gerente" (manager), and he assured me that "El Patron" would want us to stay in the guest house. His wife fixed dinner for us, and they were all charmed by the little kids. Everything turned out very well.

The next morning, we said goodbye to our wonderful hosts. We expressed our heartfelt appreciation for the help of the crop duster pilot, who gave us some free avgas and let the fence down so we could taxi over to the big field for takeoff. We will always have warm feelings about the cordial and hospitable treatment we received after our unexpected arrival at a banker's ranch on the coast of El Salvador.

***

ALMOST FORTY YEARS LATER, I had another interesting experience in San Salvador that illustrates the risks of flying small airplanes in the volatile political climate of Central America.

In 1993, my wife, Helen, and I were serving a mission for the Church in Guatemala. Our seven children were all grown up, married, and living in the States or overseas. A time of civil unrest in neighboring El Salvador exploded into a wild shooting war between the government and the Contras—right-wing rebel forces who fought against the leftist Sandinista regime—shutting down parts of the capital city and the interior. In the midst of the fracas, we received word in Guatemala that local church leaders in El Salvador had a real emergency and needed our help. They had a number of families in a section of the city that were cut off from any stores and supplies because armed groups from both sides had closed off the local streets and were shooting at each other. They had food, but what they needed immediately was powdered milk for babies. They asked if we could fly in 250 kilos (550 pounds) of this special powdered milk, as well as a list of medicines for other needy patients.

Of course, we had no airplane as missionaries, but we had friends who did, and one loaned me his small plane. We were told that the new El Salvador International Airport was right on the coastal highway where I had made the nighttime landing on a banker's ranch. The airport was under government control, so we could fly in and the El Salvador mission president would meet us with a pickup truck. Lynn Justice, a Church member and pilot living in Guatemala, accompanied me.

We loaded up and took off from Guatemala City. As we

approached the airport in San Salvador, we were above the coastline and the highway. There was a crosswind from the ocean toward the land, which meant I would have to fly inland a little, then turn back toward the coast in order to land into the wind at the airport. I called the tower at the San Salvador airport for permission to land. The tower came back immediately and said they were expecting us, and that we must land downwind.

"Do not under any circumstances circle the field to land into the wind!" the tower instructed. "The Contras have possession of the far end of the runway and they are shooting at the government troops that have possession of the terminal buildings at the other end of the runway toward the coast. They will shoot you if you fly over them!"

We obeyed and landed downwind.

The mission president met us with bulletproof vests and instructed us to wear them. The road into the city was about as dangerous as the airport runway. That night we stayed at the mission home, a lovely residence in the nicest part of town, and the mission president advised us to keep the vests beside our beds "just in case there is shooting in the neighborhood." Sure enough, about 2:00 a.m. the president woke us up.

"The shooting is coming our way," he said calmly. "Get out of bed, put the vests on, and stay on the floor until everything calms down."

We heard the shooting coming near, then it was just outside the house, then the racket moved down the street. Next, a helicopter gunship hovered right over the mission home. Machine-gun chatter, .30 caliber and .50 caliber guns overhead on the helicopter, and empty brass casings rained down on our roof. Then all quiet. The president said that the fight had moved on to another area, so we could get back in bed. We slept with the vests on the rest of the night.

The next morning, government trucks came by to pick up two bodies lying in the street and other evidence of the closeness of the action. We collected a wastepaper basket of empty shell casings we found in the mission home yard. A few cars drove by as people went to work. Next, street vendors and pedestrians appeared on the sidewalks, and everything went back to normal. Such is life in Central America!

án

Guadalajara

San Salvador

Managua

Panama City

Medellín

Cali

Guayaquil

Chapter Five

DAY 4

SAN SALVADOR → MANAGUA, NICARAGUA

W E FLEW SOUTHEAST over the lush, green, tropical fields and plantations of bananas and other tropical crops. The beach looked romantic and incredibly inviting from our low altitude before we began to climb. The morning temperature was already warming up, but our instant air conditioning began to work as we gained our cruising altitude.

Our next planned fuel stop was Managua, Nicaragua. There used to be a lovely Latin tune that began with heavily syncopated lyrics: "Ma-na-gua-Nic-ar-ag-ua is a won-der-ful-place." Little did we know that it would end up being one of our most frustrating fuel stops of the whole 10,000-mile trip from New York to Buenos Aires!

Meryl and I were delighted to successfully fly over three Central American countries (Guatemala–El Salvador–Honduras) without having to go through any paperwork annoyances. We skipped the hassles of landing at official airports, which entailed paying bribes (the price of doing business in Latin America), filling out forms in quintuplicate, wasting time waiting for officials to drink their coffee and eat their lunch, etc. Little did we know that the coming delay in Managua would cancel out a lot of our recent benefits of skipping the bureaucracy of three countries.

We landed, parked, and presented ourselves at the office, where we expected to go through the usual complicated, multi-phase procedure. The first official was immediately aware that we were American. Despite my fluency in Spanish, I had a gringo accent, and the plane bore U.S. license numbers. He sternly asked for our permit to fly our plane in his airspace. I had the copy of the telegram asking for permission and gave it to him. He said we would need approval from the Nicaraguan director of civil aviation. During our entire trip, no one else asked for such papers or approvals—nor on any other trip before or since. He was the only one to make that demand.

Anyway, my sheriff's badge did no good with him. He insisted that since we had flown in with no permission, he would have to impound our airplane and put us in jail. The only thing that saved us was having my wife and children there. He finally softened and kept Meryl, Susan, and Bobby in custody while I took a taxi into the city and talked directly to the Nicaraguan director of civil aviation. It took me about three hours to get to the office, have them dig through the telegrams they had never answered, and give me the approval with stamps and signatures—after, of course, paying some "fees."

In the end, we were cleared to continue on our trip. It was obvious that the best plan was to land at some friendly ranch, obtain fuel, and fly on south without running into ornery officials. Fortunately, this was the only such cantankerous person we ever ran into on that or any other flights in Latin America. When Nicaragua turned communist and was very anti-American, I realized that we just happened to have had the bad luck of running into one such antagonistic person on that particular day. In fact, we were lucky that we got our impounded airplane back and continued on our trip with nothing worse.

Managua

Panama City

Turbo

Medellin

Cali

Chapter Six

DAY 4

MANAGUA → SAN JOSÉ, COSTA RICA

DAY 5

SAN JOSÉ, COSTA RICA → TURBO, COLOMBIA

DAY 6

TURBO → CALI, COLOMBIA

W E WERE HAPPY to leave Nicaragua behind and delighted to be cruising at a leisurely six thousand feet above sea level, because that provided us with automatic air conditioning. The adiabatic lapse rate* cooled us off in a thermodynamic drop in temperature by about twenty

---

* "Adiabatic" means there is no heat exchange between a rising parcel of air and the surrounding air. The adiabatic lapse rate is the rate at which the temperature of an air parcel changes in response to the compression or expansion associated with the change, under the assumption that the process is adiabatic.

degrees compared to the jungle vegetation below us. Managua had been hot, moist, and sweaty, with no air conditioning in any office. The employees had fans, but no breezes were directed our way. The Nicaraguans' behavior was icy and frigid, but the environmental situation was a hot oven. Now it was different. The cabin of the plane was a delightful 70°F and the view below us was colorful and spectacular.

We had to decide where we should stop for fuel, a bathroom break, and a weather check on the scattered showers forecast for the canal. We could make a short leg of only two hours from Managua, Nicaragua, to San José, Costa Rica, or bypass Costa Rica and land at the city of David, Panama, which would take three hours. By the time we were nearing San José, there were no clouds and it seemed very inviting. We had friends who had lived in the capital and they had told us that the people of Costa Rica were very pro-American, the city is high in the hills and cool at night, and there were absolutely no mosquitos there. It all added up to the decision to land at San José.

It really lived up to the highest of expectations. The sheriff's badge worked its charm, everyone welcomed us and shortened all paperwork or just overlooked it, and there was a very nice hotel and restaurant close to the airport. Bobby slept for a solid eight hours, so we all had a good night's rest.

The weather the next morning was clear and delightful. The forecast for Panama City, however, was full of threatening showers generated by the feared equatorial front that hovered constantly from the ocean over to the coastal mountain range, and south from Panama City to the Colombia-Ecuador border. Embedded thunderstorms in that front dropped buckets of rain so heavy that visibility was zero and up/down drafts were violent.

The leg from San José down to Panama City was four hours. We had fuel for six hours but preferred to fly legs of no more than three hours. Susie and Bobby were good little travelers, but it was hard for them to stay in such a confined space for more than that. We decided to just fly two hours from San José and land at the city of David, Panama. We had heard that landing anywhere in the Panama Canal zone was like being back in the States and that we would be treated royally. We were, and it truly was a delight.

At the airport in David, we had no paperwork and all the officials were polite and efficient. We were back in the air in minutes and enjoyed our peaceful and picturesque ride down to and across the Panama Canal. We landed at Tocumen, the international airport at the Pacific side of the canal, and the officials again treated us very well. It was fascinating to see the engineering marvel of the world with its famous locks that raised and lowered ocean-going vessels. Meryl and I hoped someday to make the trip through the canal on a cruise ship from Florida to Los Angeles, California. (We did, a few years later.)

It was raining more than we wanted, but still it was light enough that we could see through it or go around the heaviest showers. It was early in the day so we decided to poke our nose into it and see for ourselves if we could handle it.

The insurance company had insisted we fly across to the Caribbean side of the Isthmus of Panama and turn south, following that coastline as it curved more and more to the south toward the Colombian border. After crossing into Colombia, we were to find a little fishing port called Turbo at the southern end of a little bay. From there we were to follow a dirt road south and then through a very narrow mountain pass into the valley between the coastal range and the next range, which was the beginning of the mighty Andes *cordillera* going all the way south to the Straits of Magellan. That valley had a lot of civilization, two big cities, lots of farms and towns, coffee fields, and sugar and banana plantations.

The two big Colombian cities are Medellín, population about half a million in 1956, and the city of Cali, population then about 400,000. We were to land at both cities and check the weather before flying back out to the Pacific Coast and on south. The Isthmus of Panama south of the canal was totally unpopulated, and likewise the coastal plain between the Pacific and the first coastal range was unpopulated. No one had ever been recovered from accidents in those two strips of jungle. Of course, we followed the insurance company's directions and flew over that impenetrable rain forest.

The rain showers over the Isthmus of Panama and further south were worse but flyable. We had no gyros for blind flying and no automatic radio direction finder, so we could never fly over the weather and then come back down through an overcast to a safe landing. We had to fly VFR all the time. The weatherman at the Tocumen airport was very helpful. He told us the front moved back and forth, northward and southward, with embedded thunderstorms that were real monsters. He confirmed that our plan to fly northward and then east over to the Caribbean side of the isthmus was the correct thing to do. He also agreed that the best way to solve our navigation problem was to go inland through the narrow pass and under the overcast south into the Medellín valley.

"Just fly through the small rain showers or around the big ones VFR," the weatherman said. "If you can thread your way from the Turbo coastal area into Medellín, fine, but if it is closed to the point that you cannot see ahead, you will have to turn around and come all the way back here to the canal. You have the fuel range to do it that way."

One ferry pilot we had talked to suggested that if the pass were closed, we could also try landing at Turbo, but he did not know of anyone who had ever landed at that grass landing field. Apparently, Turbo was not even a village—just a couple of guys with a fishing boat. The story I had heard was that during WWII, the U.S. had cleared a large area of jungle on the Caribbean beach at Turbo. The Americans removed all the trees and vines with the intent to pave a runway, which they never did. Colombia had agreed to let them construct a building with a cement pad around it and maintain it as an emergency landing site. The ferry pilot said he had flown over Turbo and it looked abandoned but useable. He had heard rumors that the Colombian military had occupied it from time to time with maybe a few troops and vehicles, which would suggest that a road is there but invisible from the air.

I did not like the idea of flying all the way to Turbo just to take a look at the pass and then fly all the way back to Panama. We had several hours until sundown. The weatherman did say that usually the early-morning weather was clear the first couple of hours around Turbo, but after that the showers built up against the coastal range, reducing visibility through that narrow pass. We decided that the worst thing that could happen if the pass was closed would be to spend the night in the plane on the ground at Turbo.

We prayed and felt good about our options, so we got in the Cessna and took off. When we reached the northernmost shore of the isthmus, just a little south of the curved neck of beach down from Colon, Panama, the port on the other end of the canal, we noticed that the rain showers offshore were lighter. Our engine was running smoothly as always, so we moved offshore a bit and flew over the water, following the curves of the beach. The base of the cloud strata was at about 2,000 feet above sea level, so we were cruising slowly at 1,500 feet and weaving in and out of the falling rain showers. Small islands appeared further offshore, like the San Blas Islands, where the indigenous Kuna people lived. We felt safe enough to continue on down the curve of the shore toward the Colombian border.

At about two hours of flying time, the coast curved around a full 180 degrees and we were starting to fly due north, which we did not want to do. (We didn't know it at the time, but we had gotten to the southern end of the Colombian bay off the Caribbean.) The rain was still intermittent so we turned inland, hoping to see into the pass to Medellín. Then suddenly we spotted on the shore below us that old WWII building with a cement pad and large cleared area. There were a couple of Jeeps parked by the building so I knew someone was there. I buzzed the field at low altitude. It looked like smooth grass with no brush except around the outside, and no animals or obstacles. It was evident that the pass was not open, and I did not want to fly two hours back to the canal, so I decided it was worth trying to land.

The moment my wheels touched the grass, I knew I had a problem. It was so deep that the prop was mowing enough grass to cover the windshield. Then I felt the wheels drag into the grass, slowing us down so suddenly that I feared nosing over. We came to a stop. Fortunately, we were at the beginning of the cement pad and by adding full power we made it out of the grass on to the pad. We taxied over to the abandoned building and shut down. The Lord was good to us again.

When I gunned the engine to pull through the tall, thick grass, the noise must have awakened, or at least stirred into action, the Colombian officer in charge of a platoon of soldiers. He came into view first and was slowly followed by about twenty soldiers in camouflage uniforms. They acted as though they had never seen the arrival of an airplane at their field. The officer in charge was young and very polite. He looked at my wife and the children with astonishment, as though he couldn't believe they were in his jungle, but he quickly got over the surprise. He recognized that our plane had a U.S. registry and asked about our destination. That was an additional shock. Argentina! In that small plane? He did not ask us for papers nor forms nor permits to penetrate his airspace. He was eager to accommodate us. A rain shower moved in, so we talked under the wing of our plane.

I mentioned the deep grass we had mowed with our prop, and he apologized and assured us he would have his soldiers cut out a swath with machetes.

"If we had known you would be landing, we would have mowed the grass!" he said. "How wide and how long do you want it?" That was generous of him to offer. I guessed we needed about fifteen meters wide and seven hundred meters long. We continued our pleasant conversation as though there was nothing bizarre about a young couple in a small plane with two babies dropping out of the sky and landing in an out-of-the-way jungle clearing. Tarzan would have been right at home there.

"Have any other planes ever stopped here?" I asked.

"Not since I have been here," the young officer answered. "But this is a new post for me. We don't always have a platoon here. There is no real port, and it is just kind of the end of the road from Medellín."

I continued the polite questioning. "Is there a town nearby? We did not see a road from the air. I guess the jungle hides it a bit."

"The end of the road is called Turbo, but I don't know why," the officer said, shrugging. "There is no town. There are some fishermen but there isn't a port per se. No ships or boats come in."

"Well, is there anywhere my family and I could bed down?" I persisted. "The building looks abandoned and the jungle looks a little threatening. The children can sleep in the plane but there's no room for my wife and me to lie down."

His answer was somewhat cautious and his tone ambiguous. "Yes, there is a place right on the beach. You can walk there in about twenty minutes. There is a muddy trail, but it is better than the road, which goes off in another direction. You'll be all right now, but don't come back until after the sun has been up for half an hour. Snakes. They come out and sleep on the warmer dirt, I guess. Then they disappear."

"You say there is a 'place'," I said. "Do they rent rooms?"

He kind of shrugged his shoulders as though searching for a description. "They have some rooms and they have bathrooms. I think someone thought there might be some tourists here from Medellín one day, but that did not happen. I think it's abandoned, but I have seen people there."

It sounded pretty fishy. However, we decided to go look at it, and if it turned out to be unsuitable, we would walk back to the plane and sleep in our seats. We moved the Cessna to the edge of the pad and screwed our stakes into the soft ground, tying it down securely. We took the portable crib, some food, and my .38. Off we went through the wet jungle, Meryl carrying Bobby and I carrying Susie. We opened up our umbrellas for the rain beginning to fall and Meryl expressed her worry about snakes in the morning.

At the end of the trail we were wet and muddy, but we easily found the "place," a concrete building that was mostly built on pylons right over the ocean. The tide was out, so crabs and other crawly things were skittering around in the mud. Susie hugged my neck a little tighter. Marks showed that when the tide was in, part of the place was over water, and when the tide was out, part of the place was over mud. We walked in cautiously. It smelled like accumulated garbage and looked half abandoned and half rundown. It looked like a setting for an old black-and-white movie with an unshaven Humphrey Bogart, a sweaty Peter Lorre—and a dozen other characters, all waiting to do something really villainous.

The unsavory-looking characters were armed to the teeth and right out of central casting, ammo belts and all. A couple of submachine guns were leaning against a table, butts on the floor. I was glad I had my own gun, but obviously I better not show it—or the badge. This was clearly a drug mafia post! We were in the middle of it. Even in those early days, everyone knew that bad guys were running contraband and worse out of Colombia. It was rumored they were heavily into marijuana and cocaine.

I worked it out that the military had been bought off and were in their place to make the drug trafficking look legitimate. They had to have been paid to look the other way and ignore what was really going on. The young officer may have been involved or just obeying orders, and I figured his part was to act innocent and let someone higher up decide whether to kill us off in the middle of the night or help us get on our way the next morning.

I had no choice but to play the part of a dumb, innocent

gringo just flying his little family down the coast. I asked the first couple of mean-looking guys in my best Argentine Spanish where I would find the manager of the "hotel."

"Che vos," I said casually. "Dónde puedo encontrar el gerente de este hotel?" ("Hey you. Where can I find the manager of this hotel?")

I added the "che vos" because Che Guevara, the Argentine revolutionary, was rumored to have been in the drug business in Colombia. The men looked at each other as if I were an alien from outer space but obviously trying to act like a lost gringo. They were stunned into inaction. That was my intent. While they were trying to connect the dots, I went on with the part I had to play.

"Estamos volando nuestro avión hasta la Argentina, donde vivimos," I explained. "Yo trabajo con el Banco Citi allá. El mal tiempo nos forzó usar su pista para pasar la noche. Mañana vamos a volar a Medellín y hasta Cali y luego seguimos mas al sur. El oficial militar allá en la pista nos dijo que aquí había un hotel. El nos mandó aquí." ("We are flying our plane to Argentina, where we live. I work for Citibank there. Due to the bad weather, we were forced to use your airport to stay the night. Tomorrow we will fly to Medellín and on to Cali, and afterwards on down south. The military officer at the airport told us there was a hotel here. He sent us here.")

One of the men recovered enough to growl, "Un momento."

He came back with another guy who looked equally rotten, rough, armed, and up to something nefarious. But he looked at my wife holding six-month-old Bobby in one arm and holding onto 3-year-old Susie by the other. I may have been a threat, but the wife and kids confused him. I don't think the place was a hotel, but it may have once been designed to fill that role. I plowed ahead, feigning ignorance.

"How much do you charge for a room?" I asked. "We just need it for one night."

"How much do you usually pay?" he said roughly.

"Oh, about twenty-five U.S. dollars."

He nodded that would be okay.

I asked about meals. He said they did not have a restaurant, but really surprised me by showing a small glimmer of unexpected humanity.

"If you need something for the *chicos* I can ask my wife to fix it for you."

I thanked him for his kindness but said we had brought some food. I gave him the twenty-five dollars.

That night we blocked the door with the bed. Bobby slept in his portable crib and Susan slept between Meryl and me on top of the one rickety bed. I did not sleep. I had the .38 loaded and ready, just in case. I imagined some in the motley group outside were arguing whether I was DEA, CIA, FBI, U.S. military, or none of the above. Maybe they were saying, "What difference does it make? Just kill 'em and hide their plane in the jungle."

After we turned off the lights, the men got pretty noisy with the kind of raucous laughter that comes from bad liquor and dirty jokes. They quieted down after midnight.

The next morning we quickly packed up and left. Not a soul was in sight. We waited half an hour to let the snakes get off the trail and into the jungle, then walked back to our plane. It was untouched and right where we had left it. While we untied it, the officer walked down the cleared area in the deep grass with me to see if it was okay. Those twenty soldiers had done a good job with their machetes. I thanked him and offered to pay for their work, but he just waved me away.

We took off, climbed to about five thousand feet, and found our way to the narrow canyon through the mountains. There was a stratus layer at about six thousand feet obscuring the peaks. It was nice and cool at that altitude. The view of steep mountain slopes with dense, green vegetation but almost treeless was a surprise. We saw occasional houses connected by worn pathways, and a few cattle and burros grazed peacefully nearby. People were scarce, but a few waved at us as though to welcome us to their private Shangri La. Before we got to Medellín, the weather cleared up and we had blue, sunny skies with a few white, puffy, little fair-weather cumulus clouds to add to the Kodachrome slides. We joked that the four-legged animals had to have two long legs on one side and two shorter legs on the other side to stand and graze the way they did on those very steep mountain sides. We wondered if the peasants collected rainwater some way to avoid walking all the way down to the river at the bottom of the canyon for water.

We made it into Medellín with no problem and stopped for fuel. I think we had burned up over half our fuel, since there hadn't been any at Turbo. We were treated like old friends with cordial hospitality, and no one asked any questions about where we had come from or where we had spent the night. No one had complex multi-copy forms to fill out.

We let Susie run around for a bit, then got back in the plane and cruised down that gorgeous and fertile green valley from Medellín to Cali. We knew we were looking at millions of coffee plants covering all the slopes of the mountains on both sides of the valley. The bottom land was wide and open and full of sugarcane and banana plantations. It was a very pretty world to watch from our point of view, about five thousand feet above sea level.

Cali was situated in an even wider valley between the two mountain ranges and not as populated as Medellín. Again, everyone seemed happy and eager to serve us. Cali was so lovely that we decided to stay the night. We found a nice hotel (with clean, sheeted beds) not far from the airport and a good restaurant.

We knew the next leg would be complicated. Cali to the coast was uninhabited and there was little civilization on down to the equator. We could fly inside the mountain range at high altitude if there were no clouds, but other pilots told us there were always clouds and they suggested flying over them due west to the coast. The insurance guy also recommended the same solution, which meant taking off from Cali in clear weather, flying over the top of the coastal range, then flying about two hours VFR on top of the low-lying stratus.

The risk, however, was the same as flying over open ocean. Below us would be solid jungle with no towns or civilization of any kind. Meryl and I considered the options before falling asleep.

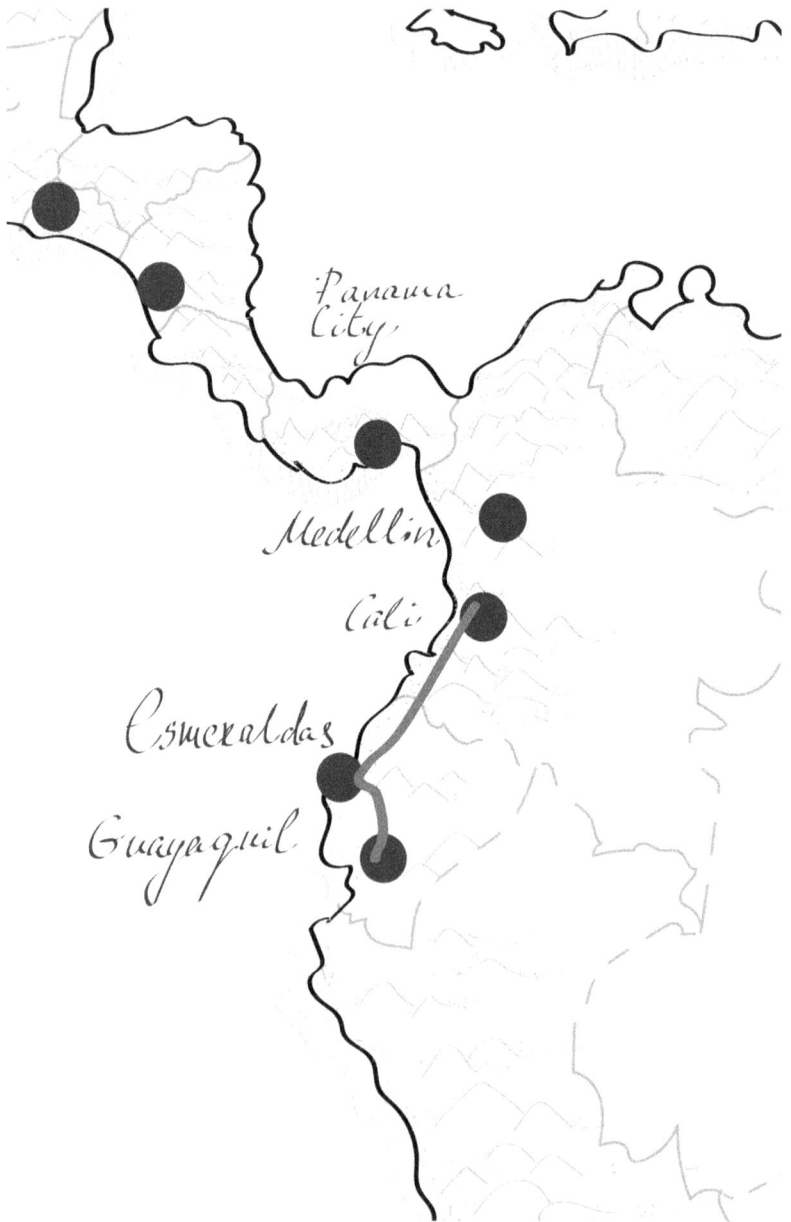

Panama City

Medellín

Cali

Esmeraldas

Guayaquil

Chapter Seven

DAY 7

CALI, COLOMBIA → GUAYAQUIL, ECUADOR

WE ENJOYED A great night's sleep in the lovely city of Cali and the new morning was fresh and clear. Not a cloud north, east, or south, but when we looked west we could see the outline of the coastal range against a deep layer of white clouds. They dropped over the low mountains down toward the fertile valley, just how other pilots had described it: like thick whipped cream spilling over a delicious dessert. The clouds were an equatorial phenomenon, and they were almost always there. The cloud layer was neither high nor dense, but extended from the coastal range to a few miles over the Pacific Ocean. Between us and the coast was impenetrable jungle. There was a thin road to the coast down there somewhere, but no way to see it through the dense foliage.

Everyone said to fly over it to the estimated coast and then turn south. They also said the cloud layer always burns off before you get to the actual line on the map that says "equator." It seemed such an important geographical landmark that I thought we might see an actual line across the beach and the jungle. The distance from the clouds spilling over the low mountain ridge to the closest beach was only seventy-five miles, less than an hour of flying over the jungle. We had prayed and felt good about it, so we took off and trusted our dependable engine.

Soon we were safely over the jungle and flying over a cloud-hidden ocean beach. We turned due south. Before we estimated we were crossing the equator, the clouds burned off as forecasted and we saw an uninhabited coastline right under us. On schedule, we were crossing the equator from Colombia into Ecuador and took a picture of what the border looked like. We decided to land for fuel at Esmeraldas, Ecuador.

Small problem: The airport was on one side of the river and the town was on the other side, and there was no one at the airport with the keys to the gas tanks. Since no one had expected us, the man with the keys had taken his outboard canoe to town. Luckily, about half an hour later we saw him coming back across the river. There were no forms to fill out and no one even asked who we were or where we came from or where we were going. I did worry about aviation gas in their old, rusty fifty-gallon drum, so I strained out any debris or water with a chamois skin in his large funnel. He had a simple

NEW YORK TO BUENOS AIRES IN 16 DAYS

wobble pump to pump the fuel. Primitive but simple.

We then took off for Guayaquil, the main port for the export of bananas, pineapple, sugar, balsa wood, Otavalo handwoven colorful textiles, panama hats, and other goods. The history of Ecuador goes back to when the Spanish conquistadores took over the northern part of the old Inca empire. The Inca headquarters were in Quito, still the capital city of Ecuador, located at ten thousand feet above sea level in the Andes. Quito, called the "Avenue of the Volcanos," is famous for the several volcano peaks visible from the city. Some are still active with occasional tremors and columns of smoke coming out now and then. The line of high, snow-covered peaks to our left stretched as far off into the distance as we could see. The Andes mountain range is very impressive.

After landing at the Guayaquil airport, we tied down the plane and filled out some paperwork. We took a taxi to what the driver called "the best hotel in town": Hotel Guayaquil. It was huge and looked very impressive. The architecture was classical Spanish colonial with lots of marble and columns, and really appeared to be the most palatial hotel we had stayed at so far on our trip. The rates were modest in dollars and very much to our liking. We were in time for dinner and the dining room served us a fine meal.

But two things should have warned us of trouble ahead. The first was the heavy odor of the port area itself. Part of the smell came from the swampy water and the garbage floating in it. The Guayas River drained from the rainforest slopes of the Andes and the melting snow up on the volcanos down through the low, flat, banana and pineapple plantations. Instead of running with some current through the city of Guayaquil, the river slowed down and there was almost no movement visible in the river that flooded out through the poorest neighborhoods. The houses were built on pylons and posts with stagnant mud under them. The level of water seemed to ebb and flow up or down a little with the changing tides. Sewage accumulated but did not wash out to sea. The seagoing cargo ships had a narrow, dredged channel and they came in slowly through the floating debris.

In addition to the smell from the garbage, there was the strong odor of coffee beans, tea leaves, chocolate beans, coconut rind, and other food that was being sundried and roasted to prepare it for export. The combination was not pleasant. In fact, it was the stinkiest place we had ever visited.

Second, when we entered our hotel room, we saw that it was infested with bugs that flew, walked, glowed, and went bump in the night. We had never seen such a collection of insects. Of course, there was no air conditioning. The heat and humidity made everything sweaty and wet, and there was no relief of any kind. The windows had screens, but they were caked with the bodies of dead and dying cucarachas so that only a little air current could move through.

The kids cried; they could not sleep, nor could we. There were at least three different sizes of mosquitoes, and they bit, stung, and sucked blood. There was running water in the bathroom, but it was rusty-colored, certainly not drinkable, and warmer than room temperature. Some of the insects flew, others hopped, some crawled. Some were big enough to be afraid of. Some seemed to come out of cracks in the floor, giving the impression that they could be followed by millions of friends the moment the light was turned off. It was a sleepless nightmare.

Sleeping in Turbo, Colombia, with the drug mafia types surrounding our room was not nearly as frightening as a night in Guayaquil's "best" hotel. In fact, one week after our landing in Buenos Aires, *Time* magazine had a report from a world-famous entomologist who declared that he was ecstatic to find inside his hotel room in Guayaquil, Ecuador, more than fifty different insects and bugs that he could capture, put into bottles, and identify and classify. We knew exactly which hotel he was talking about!*

We were all awake well before sunrise and anxious to fly off early and get up to our cruising altitude where it was smooth and cool and bug-free. Our memories of Ecuador lingered on for many years, until Citibank transferred me to Quito, where the climate was that of eternal spring, flowers in bloom all the time, and no insects.

---

* Thirty years later, our daughter Elayne served a Church mission there and reported that Hotel Guayaquil had been modernized with air conditioning and she couldn't smell the port while inside. She also didn't notice any bugs inside the hotel.

Chapter Eight

DAY 8
EMERGENCY AFTER
TAKEOFF IN GUAYAQUIL

A FTER THE SLEEPLESS night with the biggest insect collection ever found of tropical bugs in one room, we quickly checked out of the hotel and headed for the airport. It was still humid and moist, but the sky was clear of clouds and the sun was shining. There was so much humidity that the sky was not the clear blue of the desert but seashore hazy blue.

We had to wait to file our exit papers, but again, no one asked for anything complicated like a permit to enter their airspace. The flight plan was mandatory, just like in all other countries, but in the States, if you do not show up at your planned destination, and no one closes your flight plan, someone comes looking for you. In Latin America, if you failed to file a flight plan you were really in trouble, but no one would ever come looking for you if you did not show up. We had to wait to file our flight plan until the right employee arrived and finished his all-important first cup of coffee of the morning and settled into his work for the day.

Finally, we loaded the plane and took off from Guayaquil. Departure was a simple climb out over the city, an ascending left turn, then leave the traffic pattern and head across the wide Guayas River. We continued at full power, heading southward, but climbing more slowly and enjoying the gradual cooling effect of higher altitude. I set our course at a long diagonal across the river without any thought of problems or dangers. We were probably at 2,500 feet and still climbing when it happened: The engine that had pulled us through the air for so many thousands of miles with no problem was suddenly running rough and slowing down. We were losing altitude quickly.

We were halfway across the river delta without enough altitude to reach either shore. We could not turn either way to safety nor could we make it back to the airport. We had no alternatives. Our trusted engine lost partial power. Without enough power to hold our altitude, we were going to crash into the water.

The engine had been totally dependable and faithful. It had brought us all this way without a burp, shake, or shudder. We knew our 145 hp air-cooled, six-cylinder Continental engine was one of the most reputable, safest, smoothest, modern aircraft engines ever produced. Thousands of planes with those engines flew safely every day. It had the reputation of being as dependable as the engine Lindbergh had in his plane that took him safely across three thousand miles of open ocean to Paris. What in the world was happening? We were losing altitude with every second. The throttle control was pushed to the firewall!

Could something be blocking the fuel lines? I quickly considered the possibilities. It could be fuel stoppage of some sort in the two tubes feeding the engine from the two tanks in the wings. Or maybe the fuel selector valve on the floor. It was still drawing fuel from both tanks, but I quickly twisted the selector from both tanks to left tank, back to the right tank, then back to both. No change in RPMs. Part of my obligatory preflight routine that morning was the fuel system. I had correctly drained the sump at the lowest point of the fuel line system before getting in the plane and there had been no water in the collector and no visible dirt in the filter, so that was not the problem.

Then it hit me in a flash of inspiration. Maybe, just maybe, I knew what the problem was.

Back when I was a Navy cadet learning to fly at Corpus Christi, Texas, we had been trained in the remote possibility of carburetor ice, which sometimes forms in the throat of the carburetor that sprays gas into the intake system of an aircraft engine when there is high humidity. The spraying effect would chill the air and actually create ice in the carburetor throat if there was the right percent of humidity and local temperature. The ice would reduce the amount of air entering the cylinders, thus causing a lesser explosion of gas and air mixture. It would usually form ice when landing, and so as a precaution we had a carburetor heat device to apply heated air to the throat of the carburetor just in case. All airplanes of that day had enough heat to melt ice that would slow down or completely choke off the air supply for the engine.

Could ice be the problem? I had never seen it happen during takeoff nor at full power in the climb following takeoff, but I was losing altitude. I was ready to call the tower and report a loss of power midway across the delta. Did they even have boats to call for an emergency crash in the midst of the river?

Carburetor ice had to be the cause of the partial loss of power. I pulled out the heat control underneath my panel, and immediately the RPMs improved. Soon the engine was back to full power. We had only lost a part of our altitude. Meryl and I breathed a sigh of relief and said silent prayers of thanks. The children had no idea what had almost happened. We kept the heat on for another few minutes, which limited the engine to about 80 percent of climb performance, and then closed it, which returned the engine to full power. It worked like a charm. Full power was reassuring. We climbed on up to our cruise altitude.

Our trusty Continental engine continued to perform perfectly for the entire rest of the trip. But during every landing and takeoff from then on, I was ready to add carb heat if there was the slightest unexplained drop in engine RPMs. It never happened again as long as I owned the plane.

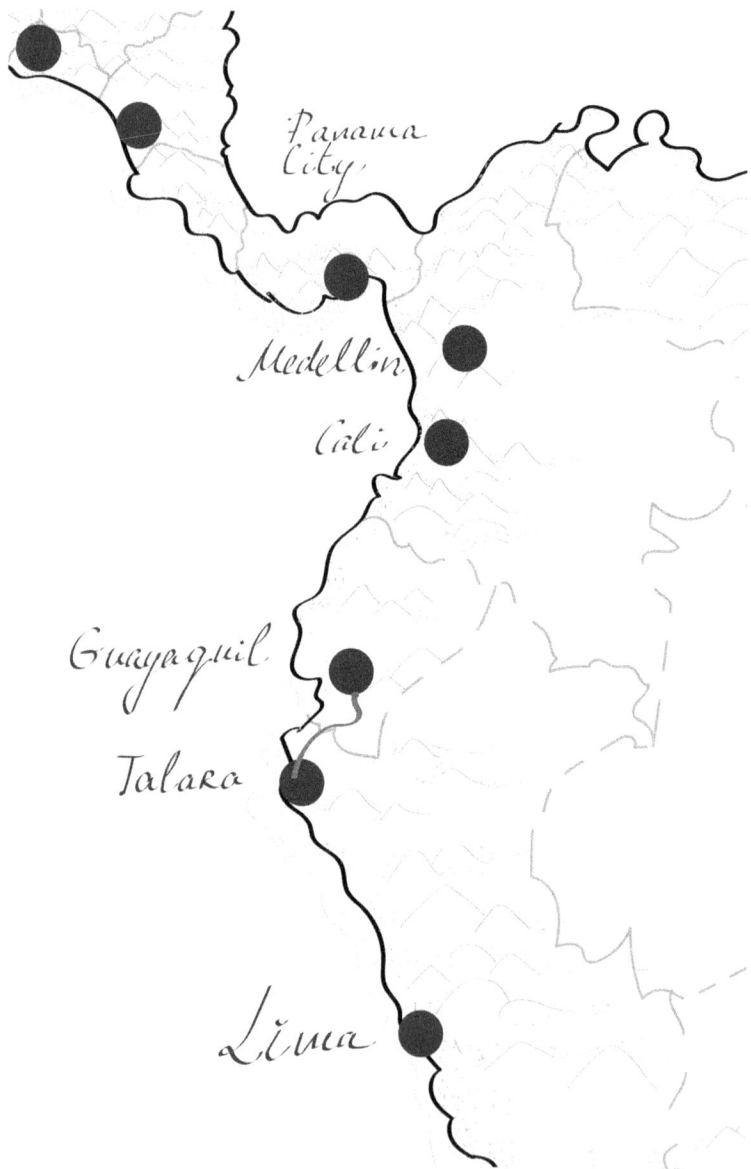

Panama
City

Medellin

Cali

Guayaquil

Talara

Lima

Chapter Nine

DAY 8

GUAYAQUIL → TALARA, PERU

AFTER THE NEAR crisis of the loss of power due to carburetor ice, we were able to climb on up to our preferred cruise level of seven thousand feet above sea level. Our course was southwest following the bulge of the coast itself for about a hundred miles over fields and very small clumps of houses, then we picked up a paved road that followed the coast and took us into Peru airspace.

Our destination was the first town in Peru that had an airport with a long, paved runway: Talara, which was a two-

and-a-half-hour flight from Guayaquil. We had been told by ferry pilots that Talara always had aviation gas. South of Talara, however, there were no airports with avgas until Chiclayo, which was a couple hundred miles farther. We had decided that a leg of four and a half hours was inadvisable, so we had to land at Talara.

We were struck by the immediate change in color of the landscape rolling out underneath us. The southern bottom of Mexico was green and tropical all the way down to the Panama Canal, fertile and inhabited with people. The isthmus was solid jungle, very lush greenery, and no people, towns, or signs of civilization. Then the beautiful Medellín/Cali valley of Colombia with big cities, highways, and lots of people, and the slopes of the mountains and the valley floor were evidence of industrious coffee farmers and big sugarcane plantations and sugar mills. That was followed by again flying over the coastal range of mountains and over the thick, impenetrable jungle, out to the Pacific Coast and down to Guayaquil, all of which was green as far as the eye could see. Now, in Peru, we were suddenly flying over desert as dry and brown and desolate as the Mojave Desert and statistically even dryer than the Sahara—less rainfall and lower humidity.

We were facing about 1,400 miles—the whole length of Peru—of solid desert. Our maps showed that the long country consisted of three parallel ranges of mountains: the western coastal range, the central range of the Andes, and the eastern range, which was the beginning of the Amazon basin with rivers running eastward all the way to the Atlantic Ocean.

We landed at Talara. The local officials were very pleasant and cordial, and paperwork was simple and easy. But there was no aviation gas! Their fuel truck had not arrived and perhaps would not arrive until sometime the following week. We could use automobile gas by going into town, buying some Jeep tanks, and bringing the gas back to the airplane, but that might ruin our spark plugs and overheat our engine. We had not brought spare spark plugs. Piura was the next major town, but they did not have an airport or avgas. We could run the risk of flying on down to Trujillo on our own tanks, but that did not sound good to us either.

We were standing in the shade of our wing trying to make up our minds what to do, when the sweet sound of a big twin-engine DC-3 on long final approach filled the air. It landed and taxied in and parked right alongside our little Cessna, which was now dwarfed by a great pioneer plane that first flew back in 1936. It was a Peruvian Air Force plane on a training flight, unannounced and unplanned. The military crew just felt like "dropping in" on Talara. They were taking turns flying and doing takeoffs and landings. They wanted experience flying into and off of as many paved landing strips as they could.

The fuselage door dropped open and out came the sharp-looking uniformed crew. I told Meryl to hold Bobby in one arm and hold Susie's hand with the other and to look forlorn. I approached the crew and asked for the captain. I explained that my family and I were on our way to Argentina and that other pilots had assured us there was aviation gas at Talara, but there was none and the fuel truck would not arrive again for about a week. I begged for twenty gallons of gas from his huge tanks. I knew it was against military rules. I explained I had learned to fly in the U.S. Navy during WWII and I was used to military discipline. But my wife and I and especially the two little kids would really appreciate a few gallons of gas and would be happy to pay for it. We needed to get to Lima.

Bless that Peruvian captain's heart! He motioned to his crew chief to bring a bucket and fill our tanks. He even had a funnel with him. The officers were generous and refused any kind of remuneration. I like to tell this little story any time I can, because too seldom do we hear of the kind and generous efforts of regular military officers of Latin American countries, particularly toward a husband and wife with two little children in tow.

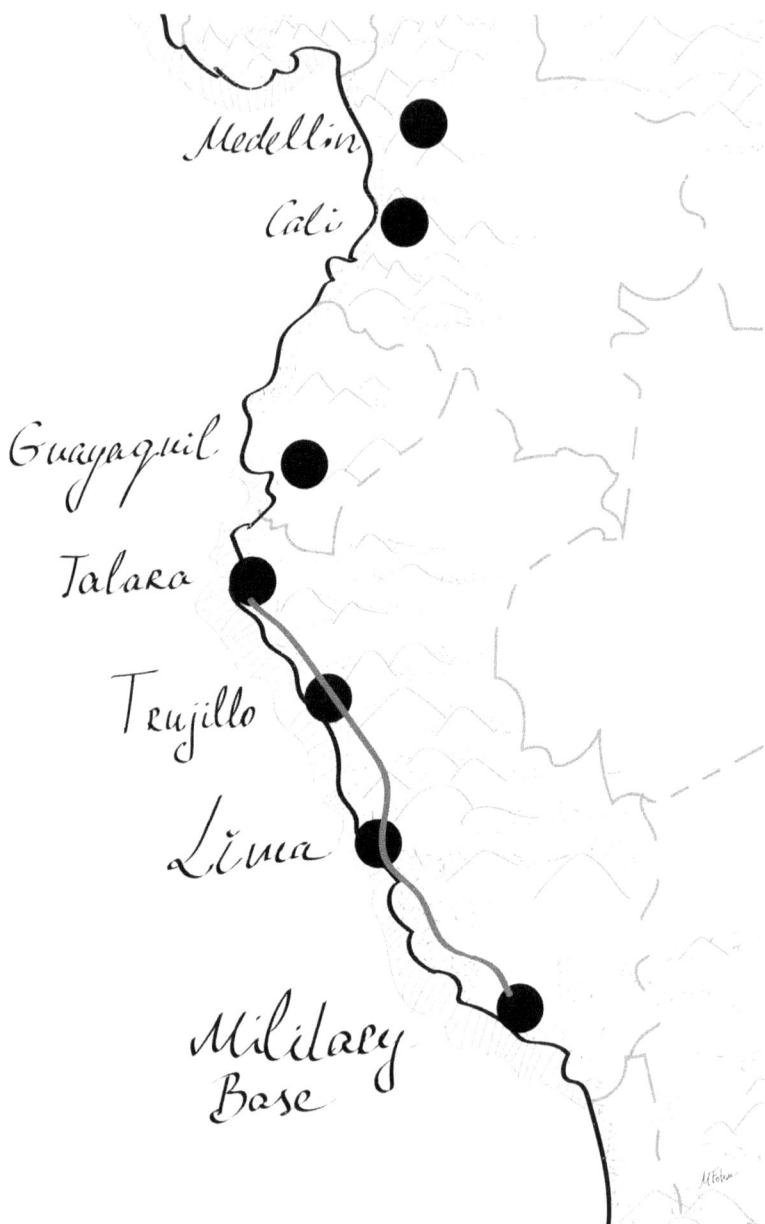

Medellin

Cali

Guayaquil

Talara

Trujillo

Lima

Military
Base

Chapter Ten

DAY 8
TALARA → LIMA, PERU

DAY 9
LIMA

DAY 10
LIMA → MILITARY BASE
NEAR MOLLENDO, PERU

THE FLIGHT FROM Talara on down the Peruvian coast to Lima was about six hundred miles of barren, brown, desert dirt. The weather was the same the whole way: blue sky, no wind. No problems and no complications. We stopped for fuel at Trujillo, three hundred miles south of Talara, and Lima was another three hundred miles down the coast. Lima is a huge, historic city with great traditions, beautiful Colonial architecture, and wonderful people. Some friends (the husband worked for Citibank) hosted us that night and we spent the next day visiting huge adobe ruins.

Going south-southeast of Lima, our route was more of the same—we just followed the coastline underneath. We saw a few mines visible with railroad tracks down from the Andes to deliver ore to a small port, but there was no need to stop except for fuel. Lima to Mollendo, Peru, was a long five hundred miles. We had enough fuel on board to make that, as there was no possible landing place in between. Mollendo would have a landing strip with avgas. We had no reserves to make a detour up into the mountain city of Arequipa.

When we landed at Mollendo to refuel, we received the bad news that, like at Talara, there was no aviation gas, and no gas truck expected for a week or so. Twice in the same country, airports that had always had fuel for other ferry pilots had zero for us. It was just the kind of thing we had feared might happen. At Talara, the Peruvian Air Force DC-3 had saved us, but there would be no DC-3 miracle at Mollendo. I was ready to run the risk of mixing auto fuel with my remaining estimated eight gallons or so in my wing tanks to get to Tacna, Peru, our required exit airport from Peru.

Tacna was only eighty miles southeast of Mollendo. The next required airport of entry was Arica, Chile, which was only twenty miles across the border in Chile. I made a mathematical calculation regarding fuel consumption. The 145 hp Continental engine used eight gallons per hour at 120 mph. But we had been flying at 100 mph, the most efficient cruise speed, burning only six gallons per hour. We had two wing tanks of twenty gallons, so forty gallons total. I made a conservative estimate that the standpipe where the fuel drained down to the engine probably stuck up into the tank an inch, which meant maybe I only had eighteen useable gallons in each tank. Thirty-six useable gallons total, and I had burned up thirty of them in the five hundred miles from Lima to Mollendo. That left ten gallons maybe, but perhaps only four useable gallons on a side. I really did not want to risk mixing auto gas with avgas, even at the ratio of two to one, to get to Arequipa or Tacna because it might force me to find new spark plugs.

Then we had another miracle. A Peruvian at the Mollendo airport said, "It is a shame you cannot land at the military airport between here and Arequipa."

I was stunned. "What do you mean, 'military airport' between here and Arequipa? There is no airport of any kind on my maps between Mollendo and Arequipa!"

"Well, it may not be on the map," he said, "but I guarantee there is a military base there. It is not very big, but it does have an airport that is just wide enough for single-engine observation planes. And there is a hangar big enough for several planes like the size of your Cessna here."

I knew military bases frequently trained with small observation planes. It might not be an airbase, but if they had a hangar and an airstrip, they would surely have avgas. The Peruvian DC-3 pilots were so kind to us in Talara, I thought maybe this Peruvian military installation would be generous enough to let us land and share some of their fuel storage with us.

It was twenty kilometers to the base—only twelve miles. Our gauges showed almost empty on both sides, but I was sure we had at least four gallons per side. We could make twelve miles and just land and throw ourselves at their mercy. The Peruvians were kind and generous. I just hoped they didn't shoot first and ask questions later.

We got back in the air and followed the highway northeast to the military post. Sure enough, there was a single strip and a hangar. We called on the radio, but no one answered. It did not have a control tower, and there was no airplane parked anywhere. There was no traffic, and the hangar doors were closed. There was no wind, so I landed straight in. The runway did not look quite right to me, but I had no choice—I did not have enough gas to circle again. I saw some tractors and trucks alongside the runway, but no one was working, and the strip was clear.

The moment my wheels touched the ground, I knew I was in trouble. I could tell it did not look like cement, but I thought it was hard-packed dirt, at least. It was not. It was very fine gravel that would serve as a base for a cement runway in the future. The small gravel made a horrible racket against the aluminum fuselage. Like the deep grass at Turbo, this stuff slowed us down a lot and soon we had trouble taxiing in. Our wheels were not big balloon tires for soft surface landings and takeoffs. The prop was stirring up a lot of fine gravel. I had to lighten the plane in order to taxi in. I stopped, jumped out, and had Meryl move over to the pilot's seat.

"Gun the engine slowly and I'll push on the wing strut on the other side," I said. "With a little more speed and being lighter, you can taxi on this gravel. Keep your speed up. You're close to the cement pad in front of the hangar. I'll walk in."

So she accelerated and left me walking in her dust. It worked fine, but it was farther than I thought. It took me at least ten more minutes to catch up with her. When I walked up to the plane, she was surrounded by soldiers. No one saw me, and I was trying to quickly think of a plan to rescue her.

However, as soon as they noticed me, Meryl exclaimed, "Oh, here's my husband!" She had been explaining to an officer that she and her family were flying to Argentina and had run out of gas. Those great Peruvians again endeared themselves to us forever. They were friendly and generous. They had never had anyone drop in on them from the skies like that, let alone a woman pilot with two small children. Plus she was beautiful and spoke Spanish with a charming gringo accent. The soldiers filled our tanks for free and waved us off into the wild blue yonder of Peru.

Guayaquil

Lima

Mililary
Base

Arica

Tacna

Antofagasta

La Serena

Valparaiso

Santiago

Chapter Eleven

DAY 10

MILITARY BASE, PERU → ARICA, CHILE

DAY 11

ARICA → LA SERENA, CHILE

DAY 12

LA SERENA → SANTIAGO

DAY 13

SANTIAGO

WE FLEW INTO Tacna, Peru, did our paperwork to exit the country, and immediately flew about twenty more miles and entered Chilean airspace at Arica. It was at the end of a long day of flying, the kids were a little fussy, and Meryl and I were tired. The accommodating taxi driver was cordial and asked if we had hotel reservations.

"No, señor," I answered. Our flight schedule had to be flexible because we didn't know how far we would be able to fly each day. "Is there a problem?"

He said Arica that week was full of Rotarians, members of an international service organization. There was a major meeting and every hotel room was filled up.

We went to three hotels and the answer was the same. We had been ready to sleep in the plane up in Turbo, Colombia, but the drug runners had made room for us. However, it looked like this time we would have to sleep in the plane after all. The two kids would be fine in the backseat area, but Meryl and I would have to sleep sitting up. We were tired, and I guess it showed.

Bless his heart, the taxi driver solved our problem.

He said, "I cannot let such distinguished international visitors as yourselves spend the night in your very small airplane. I will take you to my home!"

We tried to protest, but he wouldn't hear of it. He told us he had a small home, but it had two bedrooms and one was empty. He asked if we would help him in the United States if his family were ever in need. We assured him we would and hoped to have that privilege someday. The little home was spotless and the man's wife was very kind. They shared the single bathroom with us. Susie slept in our bed, and Bobby was very comfortable in his traveling crib. We all slept well.

In the morning, they fed us a typical continental breakfast with cornflakes, because they had been to the States and knew that Americans liked it. We explained why we didn't drink coffee, and told them about our "Word of Wisdom."* We were sure they would someday become great Latter-day Saints, because they already were anxious to serve others, even wandering pilots on their way to Argentina. We kept in touch with our gracious hosts for several years.

Our kind taxi driver took us to the airport and refused any money other than the usual taxi fare to town and back— nothing for the bed and breakfast. We discovered a lot of love in Latin America for travelers who were off the beaten track.

We continued our journey down that long shoestring geography of Chile, flying about four hours from Arica to Antofagasta. All similar geography under us: dry desert, a few mines in the mountains, and very small ports on the coast that provided services for the mines. The next leg was about five hours, from Antofagasta to La Serena. Again, desert on the coast and snow-covered Andes mountains to the east.

La Serena was our first bad weather since leaving Cali—the forecast for the airport at La Serena said there was a solid layer of clouds. We flew down the coastal highway until we met the layer of clouds, then dipped down under them but above the highway. We kept getting squeezed lower and lower underneath and closer and closer to the road. We were about a

---

* The Word of Wisdom is a health code practiced by members of our church.

thousand feet above the road by the time we got to the airport. We had flown a long distance that day.

We found a good hotel with a comfortable room, excellent food, and no problems with forms to fill out at the airport except the mandatory flight plan. In the morning, however, there was no weather service and the low ceiling looked gloomy. The weather was getting cooler—we were not in the tropics anymore. We were seeing a lot of civilization but no weather service.[*]

I finally found a local pilot at a hangar and he explained the weather pattern to me. He said the fall weather was extremely erratic. We might get stuck at La Serena or Santiago for days, waiting for a VFR flight day. Storm fronts with some rain would come up from the Antarctic starting about this time of year. The pilot said there was a front moving northward, but the front itself with rain was still south of Santiago (the city was inland from the coast fifty air miles or so). He thought the rain was also still south of Valparaiso, the big seaport for Chile. He said the local pilots flying small planes and the ferry pilots he had met get tired of waiting up to a week or so for the fronts to move through, so they had a solution that worked well for them.

I was eager to avoid a week's delay at La Serena, so I listened carefully.

He spread out my sectional map and showed me the problem and the solution. He called it a "back door" solution.

"These fronts always have a ceiling of about six hundred meters (two thousand feet)," he explained. "You can fly through a little rain on your windshield, or even a lot of rain that cuts forward visibility to almost zero, if you fly looking out the side

---

[*] Remember, this was 1956. No TVs at these little stops, no radio weather report, no newspapers with a weather forecast. We had to depend on the locals.

window at the beach road. You fly off the beach about a block or so. You will always have about eight hundred meters of visibility through the precipitation. You have to keep three hundred meters above you to the cloud base and three hundred meters under you to the surface of the water. Are you with me?"

I told him we call it "scud-running" and avoided it, but if it saved a week of waiting, I liked the idea.

"But why not fly the paved highway that way right into Santiago?" I asked him.

"That's why we call it the 'back door,'" he answered. "It's not the right way, but it'll get you there. Coming down the coast, the land rises from sea level at the coast towards Santiago, and the road goes in between some low hills as it rises. It only rises about five hundred meters, but that is enough that you will be into the ragged bases of the clouds. That is real scud-running. What we do is fly the three hundred kilometers to the Valparaiso bay and harbor over the water while looking out the side at the coast. Then we fly fifty kilometers to the next port south of Valparaiso called San Antonio. There is a major freight train track that rises above sea level, but not as much as if you come down from the north. The railroad track threads through the hills into the Santiago valley carrying cargo and you come right to the big airport of Santiago on the outskirts of the city. You never have to be more than three hundred meters above the track, and you will still be under the overcast."

"But what if I get stuck and can't get into Santiago that way?" I asked, a little concerned.

He shook his head. "Then you have to fly on south three hundred more kilometers to Concepción."

I did not feel good about either option. Meryl and I

discussed it together and decided to fly the back-door approach into Santiago from the south rather than run the risk of sitting a few days or even a week in La Serena. I had heard the stories about having to wait for the pass to clear from Santiago over the high Andes to Mendoza, Argentina, but this was the first time anyone had mentioned the problem of getting into Santiago from the coast in the low-cloud winter overcast.

We loaded up and took off. There was a light rain falling from a low cloud base as forecasted, but it was easy for two hundred miles. Then the rain became worse and it seemed that the base was lower. I was close to the Valparaiso port, flying in too much rain to see forward very well, but I was keeping high enough over the water that I could look down on the main highway traffic with all the cars' headlights on. I could not use my altimeter for the altitude because it was showing me as flying under sea level, so I knew it was wrong due to a change in the barometric pressure in the weather front.

At that instant, Meryl, who was in the copilot seat and looking sideways out of her window, shouted, "Ships!"

If she saw ships out her right side, I knew I had flown into the port of Valparaiso itself. Instead of being a few blocks out to sea, the coast had curved under me and I was flying right over the waves hitting the shore rocks. If I was now inside the port, I was headed for the warehouses at the docks. That meant I was in danger of hitting a warehouse or a ship tied to a dock. I banked hard right and turned ninety degrees.

"Too far!" Meryl shouted. "I've got a ship ahead! Back off thirty degrees!"

Now I had two ships in front of me. There was only one option: fly between them.

We wove our way between what must have been ten large cargo ships waiting their turns at the docks before we passed over the breakwater that protected the harbor. We were at the height of the cargo masts on some ships, but we were at deck level of one big ship that had not yet onloaded its heavy cargo of copper ingots, and it was riding high. The sailors below must have been very alarmed. When we cleared the breakwater, we flew straight west out over the ocean for ten minutes before turning south again. Our heartbeats finally slowed down and we breathed big sighs of relief. I estimated that we were flying about five hundred feet over the water, so I adjusted the altimeter to that.

We flew down the coast an estimated thirty miles by the clock (twenty minutes, allowing for a headwind of about ten knots, so our ground speed would have been about ninety miles per hour) and came back in towards the smaller port of San Antonio. The rain diminished enough that we had forward visibility again. We could see the port. We picked up the train tracks and followed it carefully to the outskirts of Santiago. Right at the edge of the airport we faced a new wall of water: buckets of rain! We could see the backside of the front and it truly was a wall of solid water.

I called the tower.

"I am a Cessna 170 flying VFR and following the train tracks under the overcast and I can see the end of your runway right in front of me, but I cannot see your tower nor any buildings through the rain. Do I have your permission to land and taxi in?"

The tower responded with a sense of humor. "If you can see to land, you are better off than we are. We can't even see the ground below us. Turn off the runway to your left on the first taxiway intersection and take the taxiway to the parking area.

The wall of water you mention is moving. Sit in your plane ten minutes or so and when the rain stops you can come on inside."

Sure enough, the rain moved north and we were able to park the plane and come in to the airport. We stayed at a country club in Santiago where the bank had a membership. It was international living at its best. We had friends in Santiago, and the next day they showed us around their lovely city.

Meryl and I slept that night with some uneasiness because of the challenge on the morrow. For months we had known this would be the ultimate test of both ourselves and the plane. So many planes had gone down over the Andes during the pioneering days of mail-carrying aviation company Aéropostale and the famous French pilot and author, Antoine de Saint-Exupéry.* The Cessna was smaller than the planes used by the French. They had superchargers to compress thin-air altitude so the engine would not starve. The Cessna did not. They had 500 horsepower; the Cessna had 145. We knew that the winds were bad at any altitude, even on clear days. We also knew that no matter how good the forecast was, it could suddenly turn bad. But we had talked to others who had made it across safely several times, so we were ready and hoping for the best.

---

* "Saint-Ex was assigned to South America, to take part in the opening of mail routes linking Buenos Aires with Rio, Patagonia, and Paraguay. Here, in the violent tempests and grand silence of the Andes, he found a romance every bit as potent as that of the African desert." Selina Hastings, "The Courageous, Intransigent Antoine de Saint-Exupéry," *The New Yorker*, November 28, 1994.

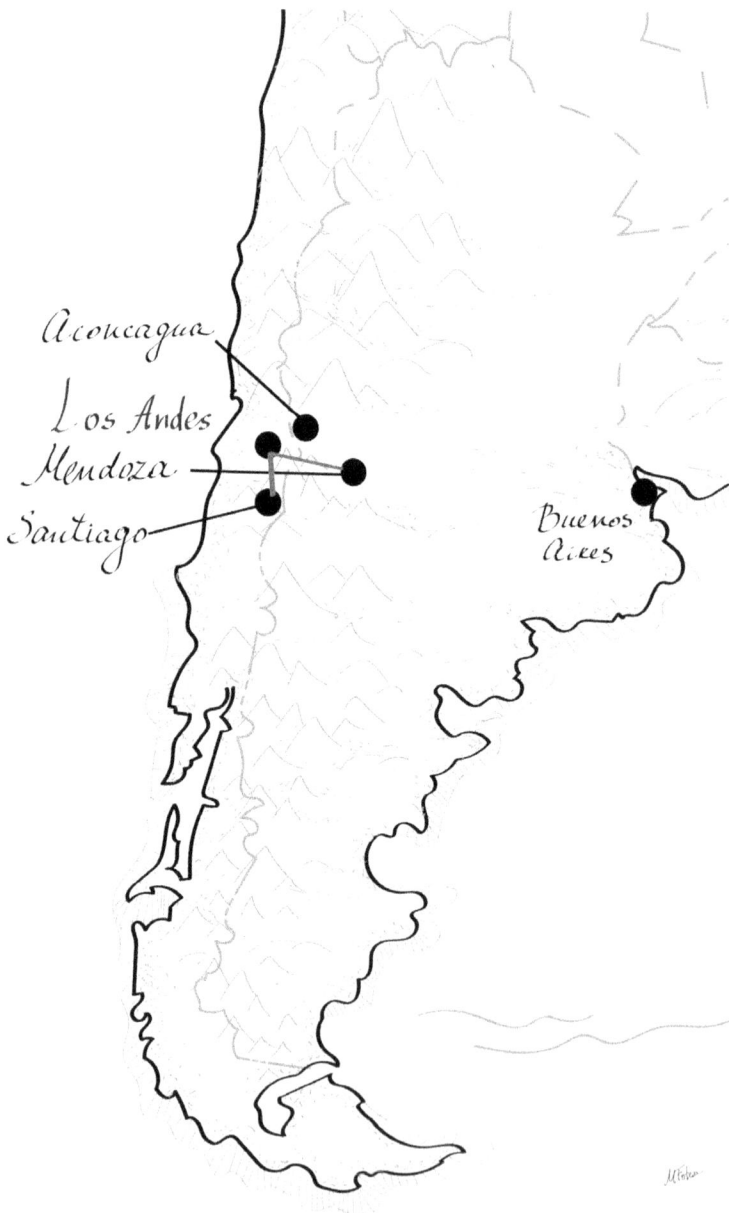

Aconcagua

Los Andes

Mendoza

Santiago

Buenos
Aires

Chapter Twelve

DAY 14

THE SPECTACULAR CROSSING

OF THE MAJESTIC ANDES

T HE NEXT DAY we got to the airport early, anxious to get going. There was some morning fog at the airport, but it would burn off quickly. The weather report was a bit mixed. The weatherman said the front had left a lot of humidity in the area so there would be lingering low clouds along the coast and some buildups toward noon. Scattered low clouds would be around the entry to the pass, but he thought we could climb over them.

"There'll be some turbulence," he said, "but I've got clear skies through the pass just for you."

He was confident we'd be able to see Cristo Redentor de los Andes (Christ the Redeemer of the Andes) as we flew over it. The statue was at twelve thousand feet and we would be a thousand feet above it. A tailwind going through the pass would help us climb to that altitude and then higher until we reached the Cessna's maximum altitude of fifteen thousand feet. Military rules are to start oxygen at ten thousand feet when you are going to climb higher. We had no oxygen tanks because of the cost and extra weight, but several aviation medical experts assured me they weren't necessary. We would only be flying between twelve and fifteen thousand feet for about half an hour.

We waited at the airport for the clouds overhead to dissipate and then we took off. We flew north over Santiago and climbed at five hundred feet a minute, aiming toward our goal of thirteen thousand feet by the time we reached the summit of the pass. To our right, we could see the towering and majestic snow-covered Andes, with lenticular clouds over the highest peaks denoting the presence of very strong winds at high altitude. We knew the turbulence would be rough because of the high winds boiling around the peaks.

We climbed up to the city of Los Andes, where both the railroad and the highway through the pass turn east and head up the gorge, then through the tunnel on top and down the Argentine side to the city of Mendoza. But to our dismay, as soon as we were over Los Andes, we saw that our entrance was blocked from one side of the gorge to the other. When the moist coastal air hits the vertical rise of the mountains, the convection effect makes the mass of air rise, and as it rises it cools off quickly, causing the moisture to become visible as low clouds. The warming sun had made the clouds grow together and expand, and they now blocked our sight. Not only that, but the tops were growing higher at a faster rate than we could climb. I tried to climb faster but quickly realized it would be impossible to out-climb the rising clouds.

I did not want to lose our altitude and fly under the bank of growing clouds and then have to climb back up. We decided to stay just outside the clouds, circling and climbing slowly until we were at twelve thousand feet. It looked like the bank of fast-rising clouds was fairly thin. I calculated about two to three miles, maybe five max. If we flew a heading on the compass for the middle of the pass, we could safely fly blind for five minutes at sixty miles an hour. And if we didn't break out into the open on the other side, I would make a U-turn and we'd wait a day in Los Andes.

Although the Cessna had no gyro compass and no gyro artificial horizon, it did have a venturi-driven gyro turn-and-bank instrument. That would be enough to hold our course straight for a few minutes at least while we flew blind up the canyon. The second hand on the clock crept slowly around the face of the instrument. One minute. Two minutes. Three minutes. Neither of us spoke, but I knew that Meryl was worried—and so was I. No rain, some turbulence. We tightened our seat belts and checked on the kids and made sure nothing was floating around in the cabin. Four minutes. Just about the time the second hand came around the fifth time, we broke through the clouds out into the widescreen vision of another world. The mists parted like a giant curtain—it was as though a celestial vision were occurring and we were seeing the other side of heaven. Here before us stretched the great towering range of snow-covered peaks of the Andes.

No pictures can describe the effect of breaking out of the clouds at thirteen thousand feet and seeing the panorama of the

gods before you with Aconcagua on the left at 22,841 feet and
Tupungato on the right at 21,555. In between were impressive
vertical cliffs, impossibly deep canyons, range after range after
range of lesser mountains disappearing about a hundred miles
to the south and a hundred miles to the north. They disappeared
from view, but in my mind I could see the map going north to the
Caribbean and south to the Straits of Magellan. We had flown
parallel to this imposing range all the way down from the
Panama Canal, and now we were crossing them.

All the peaks were jagged, sharp, saw-toothed monsters. The
range seemed to average about our altitude of thirteen thousand feet
but there were many peaks over twenty thousand, with clouds like
little hats on top of them. We were far above the tree line, so
everything was bare-naked rock. It remains to this day the most
awe-inspiring scene I have ever beheld.

Our navigation for those five minutes in the clouds had been
perfect. We were right over the highway and the railroad. The

tracks wound back and forth, into side canyons and back out, and we held a straight course far above them. Every side canyon was a dead end so we had to be careful to avoid getting trapped inside one with no room to do a 180-degree turn and get back out. To pick the wrong pass could spell disaster. We kept climbing because the close proximity of the sheer, tall peaks seemed threatening and claustrophobic, but also because the tailwind just pushed us higher and higher with no effort on our part. I held the nose level but the wind took us up. I put the nose down but the wind still took us higher.

The altitude caused the engine to slow down and the RPMs were so sluggish we could just about count the prop blades as they passed in front of us. It got so cold outside that the thermometer bottomed out and the windows frosted over on the inside. No amount of heater on the defrost position would burn a hole to see out forward. The side windows were frosting but we kept scraping at them to see out. We thought of Lindbergh—his plane had gas tanks in front of him so he could never see out the front.

We had been at thirteen thousand feet for about the half hour we expected, but now the wind had pushed us up to sixteen thousand and we were being sucked or pushed even higher. We had to get back down. I put the nose way down, and then out the side we could see the statue of Christ Redeemer of the Andes, which marks the exact border between the Chile and Argentina. I expected the wind to curl downward after we crossed the summit of the pass and take us down with it. It did not.

The two children were asleep. We didn't know if that was because the sound of the engine had lulled them to sleep, or if they were bored because their windows were frosted over, or

ROBERT E. WELLS

maybe because of low oxygen. We worried that perhaps they
had passed out. Finally we began to descend to a safer altitude.

We were down to fifteen thousand feet when all of a sudden we
hit the wildest and most violent winds I have ever felt in a small
plane. The heavy turbulence hit like a huge hammer wielded by
Thor. We heard creaks and metal strains that were frightening,
and I thought the wings might twist or bend. Rivets were
popping. Strange noises screamed out of the tortured aluminum
body and wing ribs. Then more jolts of the head-banging, teeth-
shaking kind. We had everything tied down, expecting this
phenomenon. The kids woke up startled, but neither of them
cried. Meryl gave me a concerned look—not one of fear, just
confirmation that this was what we had expected.

We looked out at the wing panels on the underside of the wing,
the only aluminum sheets we could see, and could not find any
apparent damage. Several times we tried to get down to a lower
altitude, but each time we took it back up because it was calmer
up there. We flew well clear of the base of the mountains before
we could come down safely and return to Mendoza, which we
had overflown because we could not find a way down.

We had made it. We learned that the stories of the violent high
winds in the Andes that tear the wings off planes were true, but we
had emerged safely. We had flown the width of North America
and the length of the hemisphere. We had flown across the
fearsome Andes and the plane had held together. We had worried
that the wings might be bent or ripped from their roots at the
fuselage, but they were not. We were proud of the Cessna engineers
and factory workers who had designed and produced this little gem
of an airplane. It was a feeling of great accomplishment, but at
the same time, we gave thanks to the Lord for protecting us

from our ignorance, innocence, pride, and stubbornness.

Susie and Bobby had fallen back asleep after we escaped the heavy turbulence and they did not wake up until we landed at Mendoza, a lovely, highly cultivated agricultural area on the eastern side of the Andes. It is the center of the wine/grape industry in Argentina.

The authorities were duly impressed with my sheriff's badge and treated us very well. However, we had to laugh at the dilemma we caused for them. We were U.S. citizens with both U.S. and Argentine pilots' licenses, flying a plane of U.S. registry to our home in Buenos Aires with two children who were born in Argentina and thus had both U.S. and Argentine passports. We also spoke Argentine *castellano*. They were polite, but wanted to know why we hadn't changed the registry to Argentina. We explained that we were not importing the plane (import duties were expensive) and we intended to fly it frequently to Uruguay, Paraguay, Brazil, and Chile.* The authorities finally gave up trying to get us to pay to nationalize the plane in Argentina. The paperwork was fast and easy, and after the initial questioning, we were treated like royalty returning home.

Argentina did indeed feel like home.

Saint-Exupéry tells a story about his friend Pellerin, another French pilot who experienced the same turbulence we did:

---

* We could use the plane and fly to whatever country we wanted to as tourists so long as we left that country within three months. I had received a promotion in Citibank and a transfer to Uruguay, to take place when we returned to Buenos Aires. Montevideo is just a hundred miles across the wide river separating the two countries. We had friends and bank associates in both countries, and a sailboat in the club in Buenos Aires, so we expected to spend a lot of time going back and forth in our plane.

***

HE HAD BEEN crossing peacefully the Cordillera of the Andes. A snow-bound stillness brooded on the ranges; the winter snow had brought its peace to all this vastness, as in dead castles the passing centuries spread peace. Two hundred miles without a man, a breath of life, a movement; only sheer peaks that, flying at twenty thousand feet, you almost graze, straight-falling cloaks of stone, an ominous tranquility.

It had happened somewhere near the Tupungato Peak …

He reflected… Yes, it was there he saw a miracle take place.

For at first he had noticed nothing much, felt no more than a vague uneasiness—as when a man believes himself alone, but is not; someone is watching him. Too late, and how he could not comprehend, he realized that he was hemmed in by anger. Where was it coming from, this anger? What told him it was oozing from the stones, sweating from the snow? For nothing seemed on its way to him, no storm was lowering. And still—another world, like it and yet unlike, was issuing from the world around him. Now all those quiet-looking peaks, snow-caps, and ridges, growing faintly grayer, seemed to spring to life, a people of the snows. And an inexplicable anguish gripped his heart.

Instinctively he tightened his grasp on the controls. Something he did not understand was on its way and he tautened his muscles, like a beast about to spring. Yet, as far as eye could see, all was at peace.

Peaceful, yes, but tense with some dark potency.

Suddenly all grew sharp; peaks and ridges seemed keen-edged prows cutting athwart a heavy head wind. Veering around him, they deployed like dreadnoughts taking their positions in a battle-line. Dust began to mingle with the air, rising and hovering, a veil above the snow. Looking back to see if retreat might still be feasible, he shuddered; all the Cordillera behind him was in seething ferment.

"I'm lost!"

On a peak ahead of him the snow swirled up into the air—a snow volcano. Upon his right flared up another peak and, one by one, all the summits grew lambent with gray fire, as if some unseen messenger had touched them into flame. Then the first squall broke and all the mountains round the pilot quivered.

Violent action leaves little trace behind it and he had no recollection of the gusts that buffeted him then from side to side. Only one clear memory remained; the battle in a welter of gray flames.

He pondered.

"A cyclone, that's nothing. A man just saves his skin! It's what comes before it—the thing one meets upon the way!"

But already, even as he thought he had recalled it, that one face in a thousand, he had forgotten what it was like. [...]

Pellerin began by telling how his retreat had been cut off. It was almost as if he were apologizing about it.

"There was nothing else for it!" Then he had lost sight of everything, blinded by the snow. He owed his escape to the violent air-currents which had driven him up to twenty-five thousand feet. "I guess they held me all the way just above the level of the peaks." He mentioned his trouble with gyroscope and how he had had to shift the air-inlet, as the snow was clogging it; "forming a frost-glaze, you see." After that another set of air-currents had driven Pellerin down and, when he was only at ten thousand feet or so, he was puzzled why he had not run into anything. As a matter of fact he was already above the plains. "I spotted it all of a sudden when I came out into a clear patch." And he explained how it had felt at that moment; just as if he had escaped from a cave.

"Storm at Mendoza, too?"

"No. The sky was clear when I made my landing, not a breath of wind. But the storm was at my heels all right!"

It was such a damned queer business, he said; that was why he mentioned it. The summits were lost in snow at a great height while the lower slopes seemed to be streaming out across the plain, like a flood of black lava which swallowed up the villages one by one. "Never saw anything like it before.... " Then he relapsed into silence, gripped by some secret memory.

—Antoine de Saint-Exupéry, *Vol de Nuit* [*Night Flight*] (Paris: Éditions Gallimard, 1931).

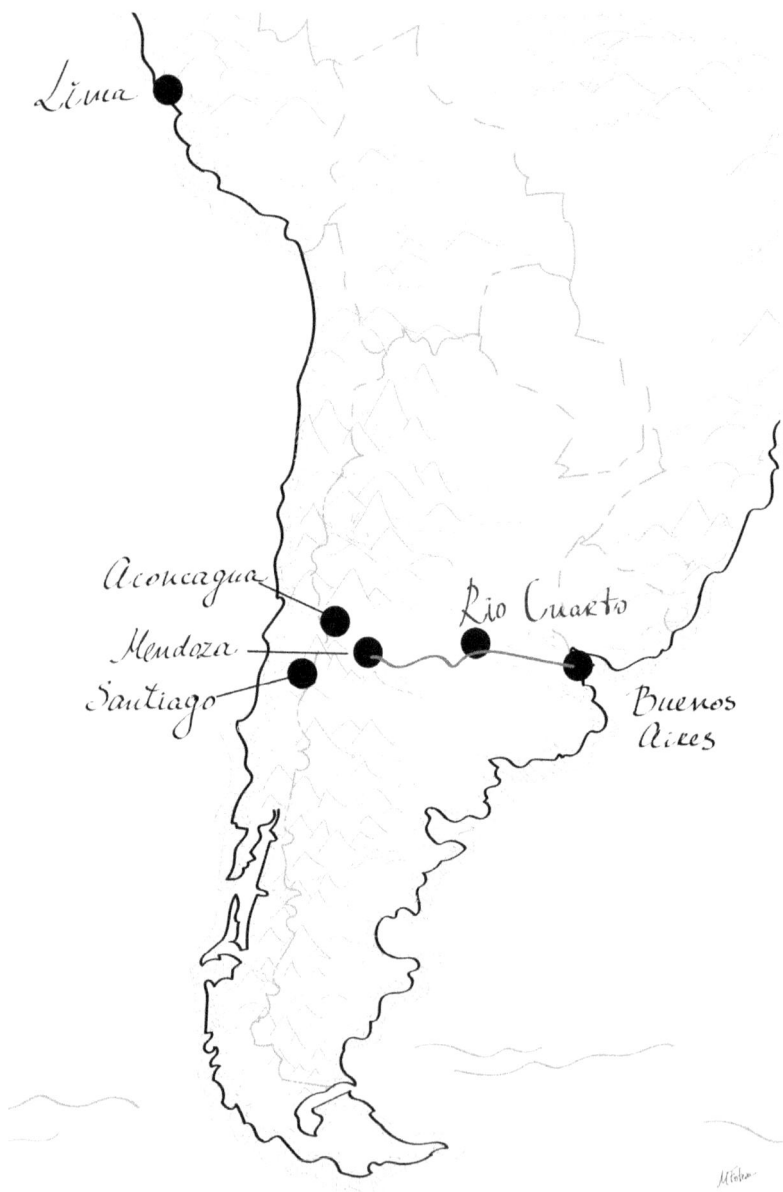

Lima

Aconcagua

Rio Cuarto

Mendoza

Santiago

Buenos
Aires

Chapter Thirteen

DAY 15

MENDOZA, ARGENTINA → BUENOS AIRES

MENDOZA TO BUENOS AIRES is about six hundred miles the way the crow flies. This would be the last leg of our long trip from New York and Las Vegas. We decided to break it into two equal parts and refuel at Rio Cuarto, where the pampa and the cattle country and the gauchos really begin. It would be a long day of flying but we figured we would be able to make it home to Buenos Aries a little bit after sunset.

We had again forgotten that we were flying due east across two time zones, so it was sundown when we left Rio Cuarto with full tanks. This last part of the flight was an anticlimax after crossing the Andes. The weather was clear all the way, and the air was as smooth as glass. The plane checked out after being tortured in the pass and the engine ran perfectly.

It turned dark well before we reached Buenos Aires, but we planned on landing at Aeroparque, right downtown on the Rio de la Plata. We radioed the tower when we were about twenty minutes out. No answer. We called again when we flew across the brilliantly lit city of Buenos Aires, a city then of twelve million people, and found that the runway lights at the airport were dark.

We radioed Ezeiza International Airport far outside the city, and they told us the lights were turned off at Aeroparque at night when they were not expecting any more international flights. We were not an international flight because we had gone through customs and immigration at Mendoza and were now a local Argentine flight. We got that taken care of while circling the dark runway at Aeroparque. Suddenly the lights on the runway came on and the tower called us and apologized. We landed, called some dear friends to come pick us up, and had a joyful reunion with them after five months of being away.

Our sixteen-day adventure had come to an end. We had spent roughly eighty hours flight time to go about ten thousand miles from New York to Las Vegas to Buenos Aires. Our estimated out-of-pocket expenses: under five hundred dollars, including gas, oil, fees, hotel, meals, tips, etc.

New airplanes increased in value so much that I could never again afford to have and operate such an expensive hobby. Insurance alone was more than I could afford. For example,

Cessna still manufactures a model 172, which is basically the same airframe with a little more horsepower and a lot more radios and instruments, and cruises at about 130 mph. It costs $400,000.

We had fallen in love with our Cessna 170. It was the best choice for us for that trip. Later, we sold a 50 percent partnership in it, and in time, we had partnerships in other planes. One was a Cessna 182, another was a Beechcraft V-tail Bonanza. Both I picked up at the factories in Wichita, Kansas. We also had a 50 percent partnership in a Piper Comanche, which was a most remarkable cruising aircraft for longer flights. We operated the Comanche 180 at normal cruise, 160 mph, burning eight gallons per hour, for an incredible 20 mpg with no wind. We had eighty-gallon tanks in it. Max Conrad, the record-setting aviator, flew a Comanche 180 from Casablanca, Morocco, to Los Angeles, nonstop. He was an exceptional pilot and it was a great airplane.

I have a little over two thousand hours as pilot in command with licenses from Argentina, Paraguay, Uruguay, Ecuador, and the United States. I have a multi-engine rating for the Cessna 310/320 and Piper Aztec-type light twins. My flying was mostly for fun, but also for charter and bush kinds of operations. I have made more than my share of mistakes over the years, so I do not recommend running the risks that I did.* But it was a great life of adventure, long cross-country flights, wonderful memories, extraordinary friends of the flying fraternity, unbelievably beautiful scenery, and exciting stories for grandkids for the rest of my life.

I close with my favorite quote from the great Charles Lindbergh:

---

* Thankfully, I learned from my mistakes. I made the same trip from New York to Buenos Aires two more times and had no problems.

I began to feel that I lived on a higher plane than skeptics on the ground; one that was richer because of its very association with the element of danger they dreaded, because it was freer of the earth to which they were bound. In flying, I tasted a wine of the gods of which they could know nothing. Who valued life more highly, the aviators who spent it on the art they loved, or these misers who doled it out like pennies through their ant-like days? I decided that if I could fly for ten years before I was killed in a crash, it would be a worthwhile trade for an ordinary lifetime.[1]

---

[1] Charles A. Lindbergh, *The Spirit of St. Louis* (New York: Charles Scribners' Sons, 1953).

I WROTE THE following article for the February 1958 issue of *Flying* magazine. Most of it repeats what I've already written, but it does have a few more details.

NORTH and NORTH and NORTH

FLYING

THE WORLD'S MOST WIDELY READ AVIATION MAGAZINE

FEBRUARY
35 CENTS

CHECK PILOT REPORT
ON THE **COMANCHE**

CROSSING THE ANDES
IN A "170"

CROSSING THE ANDES

IN A 170

A family foursome matches

a 145-hp engine and small plane against

the length of a hemisphere and

the height of the Andes, and wins.

The Wells Family is the pilot, three-year-old Susan, six-month-old Bobby and co-pilot Meryl, who learned to fly in Buenos Aires.

By ROBERT E. WELLS

HONEY, TURN AROUND so I can see it," insisted my wife Meryl. "I'll be darned if I'll let you bring me this far and not be able to say I've seen that statue."

So I banked the plane to the left and scraped the frost from the window. "Look down the wing. I'm pointing the tip right at the base of the statue."

"Oh!" she exclaimed, "now I see it. But I thought the 'Christ of the Andes' would be much bigger."

"Well," I reminded her, "it's 3,000 feet below, so it should look small."

The inside of the window had frosted over, due to the extreme cold at altitude, so I scraped it off again while Meryl held six-month-old Bobby up to see and at the same time we let Susan, our three-year-old, look out over my shoulder. "They might not know what they are looking at," continued my wife, "but some day they can say they saw it."

Being able to look down out of our own little four-place plane on the famous pass over the high Andes, where the peaceful border between Chile and Argentina is marked by the renowned Christ of the Andes, was a satisfying climax to our family adventure. We had left the States in our Cessna 170, destination Buenos Aires, Argentina, and come down the west coast of South America to Santiago, Chile, before attempting to cross the continent and the Andes.

It took 11 days elapsed time from our home in Las Vegas, Nev., to Santiago. Two days had been spent sightseeing at Lima, Peru, and another half day had been happily wasted at Acapulco. Our flying day consisted of getting off the ground as soon after sunrise as possible. We averaged four hours of flying before stopping for gas and lunch. Then back into the blue for another four hours. That way we landed at each day's destination with enough daylight to do some sightseeing before putting our tribe to bed for the night.

As we anticipated, the trip was very comparable to a two-week motor trip with a couple of small children. We made regular stops, trying to hit the biggest cities with the best hotels. A couple of times we were obliged to land at out-of-the-way places but that only added to the pleasure. In El Salvador, a ranch provided us with a splendid guest house for the night. At Turbo, Colombia, we were told of a small hotel about a mile down a jungle trail. The only disconcerting factor was the nonchalant advice not to leave the hotel until after sunrise. Poisonous snakes used the road during the night and didn't like to be stepped on!

The trip was a splendid education, the panorama ever-changing and always beautiful. Even crossing the steaming jungles of Panama, Colombia, and Ecuador, or the arid deserts of Peru and Chile, we could provide our own air conditioning by flying at a cool altitude so that our point of view was always comfortable. We weren't finicky about what we ate but for the children we had brought along canned baby foods, powdered milk, and dehydrated soups so that their diet was a constant one. We limited ourselves to drinking only bottled water or soft drinks but ate anything presented. For the baby, we had a bottle-warmer plugged into the cigarette lighter and provided him with hot milk.

The only disconcerting element on the way down was the question by everyone, "But how will you cross the Andes?" Some who had flown it in commercial planes told hair-raising tales. Pilots who had been across in big planes looked askance at our flivver and shook their heads. In Panama, one old pilot mentioned the terrific turbulence in the pass and compared it with that found in crossing the "hump" between India and China. At Ali, Colombia, the question of oxygen was raised and so were eyebrows when we said we had none. Farther along at Lima the general consensus was that our plane wouldn't even go that high! As we cruised farther south, our hesitation grew regarding the crossing we had planned, and continually projected our (Continued on page 54)

Mr. Wells is a former Naval Aviator who terms himself a "conservative" banker employed in Montevideo by The First National City Bank of New York. He describes his trip as not unusual. "We are not adventurers, nor tourists. Our only claim to novelty is taking our two children along."

25

Crossing the Andes in a 170

(Continued from page 25)

thoughts ahead to the towering mountains and the pass between Chile and Argentina where the "Cristo" stands.

We began to review our thinking to see if we had made an error in calculations. All objections mentioned had occurred to us before starting the flight and we felt that each had been solved. Frankly, we considered most of the pessimism due to lack of experience with both our type of plane and the terrain. We had flown considerably in the west where the Rockies are quite impressive and didn't feel that the Andes could be any worse. Most of those who doubted our wisdom were from areas where the land is flat. But, in spite of this type of rationalization, we did begin to worry.

The pass, according to the maps, was slightly over 12,000 feet. We had tested the plane to that altitude. The factory claimed it would go on up to 15,500 but their enthusiasm perhaps carried them away. A new model might go that high but ours with its five years and 250,000 miles was far from being new. And what if we really needed that extra altitude?

The question of oxygen had worried us because of the babies. Their health had been good on the trip and they had behaved well but would the lack of oxygen at altitude make them sick? Normally, in military flying, you start using it at 10,000 feet. We might have to go half again as high. The argument in our favor was the length of time we would be at that altitude. I estimated a maximum of 30 minutes. We could climb into the pass gaining altitude and, as soon as we crossed over the summit, could begin to let down. Total time above 10,000 might be half an hour. We had, of course, consulted a physician whose opinion was that no ill effects would be felt for such a short time. The turbulence to be expected didn't bother us too much, as we had planned on making the flight only on a day with ideal conditions.

The day finally arrived. After a good night's rest in Santiago, we were ready to tackle the most important leg of our journey. Weather reports from the pass were good but we were delayed at the airport by a bit of local fog. We waited impatiently until ten o'clock, when we received clearance to take off. The towering Andes, with their snow-capped tops, were impressive as we started the long climb to conquer them. We had 70 miles to fly parallel to the range before we would come abreast of the pass.

Our plan had been to get 10,000 feet before arriving at the mouth of the canyon and then climb into it, gaining the other 2,000 feet between there and the summit. But shortly after taking off, it became evident that there were small clouds blocking the entrance. By the time we arrived opposite the pass, the clouds were bigger and completely obscured the mountains. Apparently, weather had changed radically since our earlier report from the summit. But there was a chance that this was just a cloud bank on the

near side of the mountains and that the pass was still clear. If we could get higher than the clouds, we might be able to see through. We decided to keep on climbing, while holding our position by doing lazy circles. It looked as though the top of the clouds should be at about 12,000 feet and we were already at 10,000. Perhaps the build-up would be impossible to top but it was worth trying rather than go back to Santiago immediately. We finally hit 12,000 and could see holes through towering pillars of clouds whose tops were away on up. The clouds were mounting faster than we could climb.

As we crossed back and forth over the mouth of the pass with the cloud bank between ourselves and the mountains, we

**NEXT MONTH
IN FLYING**

◆

**T-EFFECT . . . A NEW
PHENOMENON**

An elusive "air cushion" that exists only in a narrow band of altitude above the sea materially aided a crippled C-97 to remain airborne for six hours over the Pacific before ditching.

◆

BARNS INTRIGUE ME

Tracking down old airplanes can be a fascinating hobby. The author found a 1911 Thomas Pusher, piece by piece, and then the pilot who originally bought and flew it.

◆

SALUTE TO PHOENIX

A municipal school system that has given more than 28,000 hours of flight training to its student body sets a fine example for air age education.

◆

FROM KANSAS TO COSMOS

Flying the Spanish Main was the interesting assignment of an Air Force pilot from the Kansas prairies, when he operated an amphibious SA-16 supply line along the guided missile range.

began to doubt that we could make it. We had already been above 10,000 feet for 15 minutes and would have to spend at least 30 more going across but we were almost up to 13,000 and it looked like there might be a good hole opening up. Suddenly, there was a break in the clouds and we could see the pass! The mountains beyond were clear of clouds all the way through to Argentina.

Blue sky all the way across! We turned toward the hole and started in. Suddenly the winds stirred the clouds and they

swirled around us. We found ourselves half way through the cloud bank headed directly for the mountains but with no hole. We held a straight course on instruments for what could not have been more than 20 seconds but our anxiety was terrific because of our proximity to the peaks which were immediately in front of us. I was ready to do a 180 and get out of there when we broke through.

Never had we beheld such a scene. The view had been obscured by the clouds building vertically and now it was as if celestial curtains had been parted. Before our eyes lay the most magnificent scene imaginable. Wild, sawtoothed, snow-covered peaks extended to left and right and off into a mystic horizon. We had flown in the mighty "Rockies," seen photographs of the "Himalayas," but never has there been anything to compare with the awesome Andes. Seeming vibrantly alive in the brilliant sun, they thrilled us beyond words. The ruggedness is fearsome, yet enchanting. The coloring is spectacular.

The pass was right in front of us, so we began to thread our way through the peaks, following our course closely on the map and checking constantly. Following the tiny thread that was the railroad track, we almost flew into a blind canyon before we noticed that the track came back out again and went into another. We were at 14,000 now but the walls of the pass were still higher and the ground was getting closer, so we kept on climbing just to make sure. It was only a few minutes before the summit came into view and, by the time we passed over it, we had our full 15,000 feet and were sitting on top of the world.

It was so cold that we had to keep scraping the frost off the windows. Our moist breath condensed on the glass and froze immediately. I would scrape a hole on my side and have Meryl lean over to see my view. Then she would clear a peek-hole on her side and I'd look at her scenery. The size and grandeur of the mountains was so overpowering that I felt they were much closer than they actually were. At first I was afraid to turn the plane because the peaks seemed so close. As we became used to such magnificence and calmed down, it became apparent that we actually had more than enough room and could make complete circles in the pass with space to spare.

As high as the mountains were, it appeared impossible for nature to pierce the sky with anything greater, yet as we approached the summit we could see, off to our left, the towering glory of Aconcagua, the highest peak in all the Americas. No vocabulary can describe it. We just sat and looked at it in silence as we passed by. The beauty was actually a spiritual experience and we felt elevated by it. It seemed especially fitting to hold the children up to the windows and make a slow turn over the statue of Christ!

I must admit that we were a bit exhilarated. We had matched our 145 hp engine and small plane against the length of the hemisphere and the height of the Andes and had won.   END

I have been an avid, cover-to-cover reader of your fine magazine for well over 50 years. In fact, in your February 1958 issue you published an article of mine titled "Crossing the Andes in a 170." My article was about a trip of mine from New York City west across the continent to Las Vegas, my birthplace and the residence of my parents, and then down the west coast to Chile. From there we flew over the Andes in the "shadow of Aconcagua" and east to Buenos Aires where I had been stationed by my employer. I just wanted to report to you that I am still alive; have made the trip from Wichita to deep South America in a new 182 and a new Bonanza.

ROBERT E. WELLS
St. George, Utah

Flying magazine, "Flying Mail," April 2008.

ADDITIONAL FLYING STORIES

BOLIVIA

BRAZIL

Chaco Paraguayo

PARAGUAY

Asuncion

Villarrica

Ciudad del Este

Foz do Iguacu

ARGENTINA

Story One

THE MERCY FLIGHT

I N ORDER TO appreciate the risks of this story, let me describe two incidents which illustrate the problems of living in a Latin American country that has a heavily armed military and police organization. The armed men are frequently only very young conscripts doing their obligatory military service and blindly carrying out strict orders. At every military base—some of them are inside cities—the orders are that every morning and evening, as the flag is raised or lowered, all vehicle traffic must halt in place until the bugle finishes blowing and the flag detail marches off. Orders state that if any vehicle does not stop out of proper respect for the ritual, the armed guard will fire a warning shot into the air, and if that does not stop the vehicle, the guard will fire at the car.

In the hot tropical city of Asunción, Paraguay, the moment the sun casts its very first rays, it instantly becomes very hot. Everyone drives with the windows open and the breeze blowing. One morning, a foreign driver who did not know the local rules passed in front of a local military base when the flag ceremony was going on. He was driving a new car with air conditioning so the windows were up, he and his passengers were talking, and the radio was playing music, so they didn't hear the first warning shot and drove on. The guard fired at the disobedient car, tragically killing a Catholic nun sitting in the rear seat.

On another occasion, a military officer serving in his country's embassy was driving recklessly, failed to stop at a clearly marked stop sign, and barreled through a busy intersection, narrowly missing another car. Two uniformed policemen parked on their motorcycles sped off after the offender. They pulled him over to the curb with red lights flashing and sirens blaring and ignored the embassy license on the car. The driver sat angrily in his car, demanding respect for his diplomatic license, which to him meant that he had the right to speed through any sign with total impunity. The police didn't care who he was; they had been instructed to apply the law to any driver who disobeyed a clearly marked sign and endangered other vehicles and/or pedestrians. The foreign embassy officer, with loud disgust, made a nasty remark about the police officers' intelligence and their mothers. One of the policemen executed the offender on the spot.

Drivers new to a South American country heard these stories as a cautionary tale about obeying the military and police at all times. Expats also warned the new drivers that most people carried sidearms in their glove compartments. Many were cattle ranchers and there was a lot of cattle rustling going on, and others were just normal citizens wanting to protect themselves. This was like the Wild West. One year I lost three bank clients, including an American, all killed in gun battle shootouts. Expats suggested to newcomers that it was not wise to lose one's temper over a traffic fender bender or because someone cut you off, because there had been cases of two drivers resorting to an armed duel before the police even arrived at the scene.

***

WITH THAT AS background, let me tell a story. One day at the bank in Asunción, a very worried Protestant minister came to my office and pled with my secretary to let him see me. He was not a client of the bank and did not want a loan, but he had an emergency and insisted that I was the only one who could help. My secretary escorted him into my office.

"Mr. Wells, I really need your help!" he began. "Because of the threatened invasion from across the border by the opposition political party, all civilian airplanes are grounded."

"Yes, I heard the news," I said. "But what can I do to help you?"

"We just received a radio call from our Chaco mission about a hundred miles away. There's a woman there who's very ill and in need of immediate surgery. We have to get a plane out there to bring her in, or else she will die. We know you are a man of faith and that you are a lay minister and the head of the

Mormon Church here. We also know you are a pilot and you have a plane, and we understand that you have a lot of influence with local authorities. I have been led by the Spirit to ask for your help to save this poor woman's life."

The minister was anxious and sincere and pled for my help. I was the district president so I was indeed the leader of all branches of the Church in Paraguay. I had the clear impression I was supposed to help this minister. I immediately called my friend who was the head of civil aviation for the country. In fact, he had signed my Paraguayan pilot's commercial license so I could do charter flights on Saturdays when the bank was closed. I considered him a personal friend. I explained that I knew there was a critical political situation unraveling and that all planes were grounded, but I needed his permission to fly my plane to the Chaco to save a woman's life. My friend was sympathetic but said that the presidential order grounding all airplanes would be in place for a day or two. I responded that the doctors said the woman would die in five hours if she did not have surgery in an equipped hospital.

"Bob," he said patiently, "no matter how close we are as friends and colleagues, this is a presidential order and armed guards are by every hangar and every plane outside. There is no way I can override that order. Why don't you try the general who is the commander of the Air Force? You've flown with him. Maybe you can get him to help you. I'm sorry, but there is nothing I can do."

I told the minister to keep praying and called the general, a good friend and client. I explained the critical situation.

"Bob," he said sympathetically, "I truly am sorry, but it is out of my hands. Everything is locked down by order of the president. You'll have to call him to get permission."

I looked at my anxious visitor and told him I'd exhausted

my options. I could not interrupt President Stroessner during such a crisis.

The minister persisted. "I know I have been brought to you for a reason. There will still be a way."

I felt his faith and it encouraged me to go to the president.

I called his office and, as expected, his secretary answered. She knew me but said she could only put me through to the assistant to the president because President Stroessner himself was in an urgent meeting with his generals. The assistant also knew me and said he would go into the meeting and if he had a chance he would tell the president that I had a personal emergency. But after a few minutes he came back on the line.

"I am so sorry, Mr. Wells, but the situation is tense enough that I could not break in. You must let her die."

I turned to the minister at my desk, ready to apologize, but then I had another idea. It had to be inspired.

"Out on the far side of town is a small grass runway and two old hangars," I said. "Maybe they have forgotten the Air Club. I gave them a loan to buy a used Stinson, and the club told me I could use it any time I wanted. Let's drive out there and see if the plane is outside."

The minister and I drove out to the Air Club. As we approached the hangars, I noticed that the Stinson was parked right where it should be, and it was not even tied down. There were some military guards on the far side of the hangar, but no one was close to the old, faded green high-wing Stinson.

"I'll get in on the pilot's side, and you walk quickly to the other side and climb in. By the time you get in your seat I'll have hit the master switch and starter switch and hopefully the engine will catch immediately."

When I hurriedly got into the plane, I glanced at the fuel gauges just to make sure we had full tanks. But before I could release the brakes, an Air Force officer came running. I knew him—I had flown with him in a twin Beech cargo plane once. He was waving and shouting. I started the engine and revved it up. The officer pulled out his pistol while running and pointed it right at me.

Then I did something from clear inspiration. The RPMs of the engine and motion of the propeller were stirring up just enough wind that he did not come closer. I held my left hand out the window and used sign language that is understood around the world. I formed a gun with my thumb up like a pistol hammer and my index finger straight out like the barrel of a pistol, pointed at the engine, and made the motion of shooting. Then I took my other hand off the throttle and pointed that index finger at myself, shook my head, then pointed at the engine also. Both my index fingers were pointing at the engine.

I prayed that the officer with the real gun would get my message: "Don't shoot me. Shoot the engine instead!"

I saw the perplexed expression on his face as he understood my message and stopped running. I immediately pulled my right hand back inside, increased the RPMs, released the brakes, and added full power. We sped down the runway with our backs to the officer and took off. He did not shoot.

We stayed very low to avoid detection. If anyone had seen us, a fighter pilot would come after us and shoot us down without hesitation. I was sure the faded green fabric of the Stinson would be impossible to see from above against the green foliage of the Chaco fields and pastures.

We made the flight and picked up the very sick woman, who

had to sit upright for the hour flight. I radioed into the tower for an ambulance. We landed at the main airport, still bristling with armed guards everywhere, but we got her into the ambulance and it sped off toward the hospital. The reverend and I left the Stinson and took a taxi back to the bank. I sent a couple of employees out to the Air Club for my car. The reverend called later to tell me the operation was a success and thanked me profusely.

I heard from other Air Force officers that the incident had been reported to President Stroessner, but he just shook his head and said to leave me alone. However, he did order the Air Force to give the officer who did not shoot me a one-month penalty of house arrest.

About three months later, I saw that Air Force officer at a party, and I thanked him for not shooting me.

He shrugged and shook his head slowly. "I was an officer under orders so I should have shot you or your engine, but I'm a pilot, too. When you made that hand signal to shoot the engine and not you, I just could not ruin a perfectly good airplane engine."

THE CONTRABAND FLIGHT

WHEN WE MOVED from Uruguay to Paraguay to open a new bank in Asunción, I found that Paraguay had only one paved road, which went east for a hundred miles. And, of course, it's landlocked. In order to solve the problem of communication for businesses (many outside the capital city did not have phones), to bring emergency patients to hospitals to Asunción, and to allow political leaders to manage the country, Paraguay was full of grass and dirt strips for single-engine airplanes. Bigger towns had a few dirt strips for DC-3s and twin-engine Beechcraft-type aircraft.

The dozen or so qualified pilots in Paraguay were very much in demand and treated with great respect and admiration. Many of the large ranches had their own airplanes flown by the owners, their sons, and a few hired commercial pilots. The definition in Paraguay of a "large ranch" meant a hundred thousand acres up to one million acres, with a number of dirt strips strategically located close to water sources and corrals on site.

I had no plane of my own at the time we arrived, having sold the Cessna 170 we flew from New York to Buenos Aires. My plan was to buy another plane in the States and fly it down to Paraguay, which I did later. Within the next two years, I flew both a Cessna 182 and a V-tail Beechcraft Bonanza and was part owner of each.

Flying in Paraguay was a problem in that there seemed to be no map of all the dirt strips in the country. Each pilot had his own map either in his head or on a notebook, but just for his own immediate area or common routes to and from Asunción. I could not find a map showing the entire country. Paraguay was small compared to Brazil and Argentina, but it was still a significantly large piece of real estate. It was six hundred miles long and three hundred miles wide at the northern end and two hundred miles wide at the southern end—about the same number of square miles as California. The northern end shared a border with Bolivia and Brazil, while the southern end bordered on Argentina. Uruguay and Paraguay did not share a border, as a small portion of Argentina divided them.

As a banker with clients throughout the whole country, I needed a complete map. I wanted to be able to count cattle as collateral at the bigger ranches, count bags of sugar at the sugar mills, count bags of quebracho extract at the mills (used to tan leather for export to the U.S. and Europe), count logs of valuable hardwood in river ports in large rafts waiting for export to saw mills in Argentina, and view tons of canned corned beef at the three major canning plants, along with raw tobacco, coffee beans, vegetable oils from coconuts, and petit grain used in perfumes. We specialized in financing exports from Paraguay, as well as imports of vehicles, tractors, factory equipment, computers, and accounting machines, and even silk articles from China and the Far East.

Another pilot gave me an idea. He said there was one company that offered small airplane service to the whole country. They operated small, four-place, single-engine planes as well as light twin-engine planes (all war-surplus Beechcraft AT 11s that carried up to ten passengers and one ton of cargo), taking off from dirt or grass strips to and from every corner of the country. He explained that this company was actually a private business owned and operated by the Paraguayan Air Force pilots. The officers owned the planes and flew them in their off-duty time. He said some of their pilots must have landed at every ranch, town, mill, and business in the country and they surely could help me make a map of all the major airstrips. All I would have to do is make friends with the Air Force general in charge and get his approval.

I visited the Air Force general and we talked flying, then business, and he became a client of the bank. He agreed to instruct his pilots flying the twin-engine planes to take me with them as co-pilot on Saturdays and point out every airstrip in the country. It was a tremendous help, and I was able to make my own map after a few flights.*

One Saturday I flew north, the next I flew south, and the next I flew east. I never flew west, however, because Asunción is very close to the western border that separates Paraguay from Argentina. I had each pilot point out major landmarks such as the color of a river—red, green, muddy, etc. The towns were easy, but some strips were invisible, so I wanted to know if the strip was on the north, south, east, or west of the town. I kept full notes for a long time. Some mills had smokestacks for large boilers and steam engines to run for power and others had diesel generators. Some ranches had fifty to a hundred miles of railroad and steam locomotives and others had modern diesel systems. I learned that some ranches had nice homes, while the owners of others lived in the city and rarely even stayed overnight at the ranch.

The pilots were all friendly and competent, and their mechanics took great care of the engines and props. The planes themselves, however, were getting kind of worn and needed maintenance. They often used bailing wire to fix them. One time, the fabric-covered aileron on my side tore off in the slipstream. We were flying at about 170 mph, and flew back to Asunción with tape holding part of the fabric in place. A while later, that tore off also.

The radios and instruments weren't fixed because the pilots seldom flew instruments, and spare parts for the instruments and radios were very expensive or impossible to obtain.

One Saturday morning, I wanted to fly east. I particularly wanted to fly to Hernandarias, a city right on the Paraguayan side

---

* My son David has a copy of that map. It was hammered into a large sheet of wet cow hide and eventually embedded into a coffee table.

of the Brazilian border. It was also the route to Iguazu Falls. I had been to Coronel Oviedo, a city right on the road going east to Brazil and Iguazu, but that was only halfway to the border. I had been north to Pedro Juan Caballero, the coffee capital of Paraguay, and south to Encarnación, the yerba mate capital of Paraguay, but had never been to Hernandarias.

I had heard that from there you could see the rising column of spray from Iguazu Falls, but the falls themselves were located just a few miles away where Brazil and Argentina shared half of the falls on each side of another large river. The three countries joined together where the Iguazu River flowed into the much larger Paraná River. I knew that many tourists came to Paraguay and took a very bad road to Hernandarias (200 mi.) and then crossed the Paraná River in a rowboat and hired a taxi to take them out to the falls on the Brazil side of the river.

I could fly people to Hernandarias and back to Asunción in the same day. At that time, to fly from Paraguay into Foz do Iguaçu, the city on the Brazilian side of the falls, you had to request a landing permit, which took three days to get approval.

That Saturday morning when I arrived at the operations office, there were flights scheduled to the north and the south, and also one to Hernandarias. I was delighted. I found the pilot, a lieutenant, and told him I was his co-pilot. He was not as warm and friendly as other pilots had been, so I figured he was having a bad day or maybe had been passed over for promotion. I reminded him that the general had given me approval to go on any flight with any pilot.

"I'm actually loaded a little over gross weight, so I don't think today would be a good time," he said tersely.

I had looked in the plane and it was full of wooden crates,

so I knew he was probably right, but the twin-engines were Pratt & Whitney radials—R-985s, 450 hp each, famous for full power and total reliability. I weighed two hundred pounds. The cargo had to weigh slightly over two thousand pounds. But we had ten thousand feet of paved runway for takeoff, so all we had to do was add maybe a few hundred feet longer for the takeoff run. We were returning empty, so I insisted I wanted to be his copilot.

He had one other excuse, something about having to add a passenger manifest in quadruplicate.

He mentioned that the engine on my side was throwing a little bit of oil so I would get my shirt dirty. That did not bother me either. He gave up. I did not take any of his hints.

He said, "Okay. Get in. You like to fly, so it's your plane."

I started the engines and taxied out. The radio was not working so the tower gave us a green light. I pushed in the twin throttles, advanced the prop controls, and we rolled down the runway. It did take us a little longer to take off than normal, but those nine hundred horses pulled well, and we lifted into the sky before a third of the runway was under us.

We climbed to a low cruising altitude and settled into a slow cruise of about 160 to 170 mph. The distance to Hernandarias was some two hundred miles and the route was a straight road to the east. A North American construction company was widening the road, putting down a hard-packed base, and applying a black top paving to it. The road was already paved from Asunción to Coronel Oviedo, but it was red dirt through the jungle the last hundred miles. We were flying with our windows wide open. Those big Hamilton Standard props were very noisy, and the tips were very close to our ears. We could not even talk to each other. At about fifteen minutes from Hernandarias, and with the column of mist from the falls very visible to us, I came back on the throttles to begin the gradual letdown.

Without saying a word or making a signal, the lieutenant reached over to the throttle quadrant and pushed them back into full power. Then he raised his right hand, flat and vertical, and motioned that we were going straight ahead.

I was confused. "Hey, it's time to let down!" I shouted.

He repeated his hand motion indicating "straight ahead."

I yelled, "That's Brazil!"

He nodded but did not look at me.

I motioned towards the cargo behind us with my thumb and yelled, "Contraband?"

He nodded his head, took out his automatic pistol from the holster, and placed it over on his side of the windshield under the plexiglass. I had heard the rumor that some of the Paraguayan Air Force pilots were supplementing their modest salaries from time to time by flying contraband into Brazil and Argentina. Now I understood his reluctance to have me fly with him on this run.

All I could do was fold my arms and yell in his ear, "Your plane, sir!"

I could see the newspaper headlines: "Prominent U.S. Banker Arrested Flying Contraband into Brazil!" I wondered if anyone would believe my story that I was an innocent bystander.

He flew us right over Hernandarias and the Paraná River and a little to the north of the city of Foz do Iguaçu. We continued directly east about twenty minutes, flying over heavy jungle. Then he circled the plane over a big clearing of grass. Men came out of the jungle shade and placed a bed-sized white sheet on the ground. He circled into the wind and landed, but kept the engines running. A truck came out of the jungle to the side of the plane. The pilot left for a few minutes after the cargo was unloaded and, I assumed, returned well paid.

We were very light going back with no cargo. He took off, this time downwind, climbed quickly to altitude and headed back to Hernandarias. I kept a nervous watch out the window to see if the Brazilians had sent fighters to intercept us. None appeared. I still worried about possible newspaper headlines. We landed at Hernandarias—I assumed he had to have some evidence we had landed there. The airport keeps a record of every plane that lands and takes off.

The pilot asked if I wanted to fly home. I felt I had endured enough guilt of conscience, so I turned him down.

That was the only time I ever transported contraband, and I never flew with another Paraguayan Air Force officer again.

Story Three

THE NAVIGATION FLIGHT ERROR

I LEARNED A LOT about flying from this near-accident experience. When flying a new plane, a pilot can never assume he's familiar with it just because he's flown something similar. It's dangerous to think you know all about a particular plane, especially when it is an older model that has been through a lot of bush flying. For example, I love Cessna 180 tail-draggers of any vintage, with any equipment, or any background, to the point that one time I was overconfident and felt safe flying a plane without asking its owner any questions.

One Saturday morning I was wishing I had a plane to fly. I would go anywhere. I had sold my first plane, the Cessna I had flown from New York to Buenos Aires. We had moved to Paraguay and I was really itching to fly and get to know the country. I had met the director of Paraguayan civil aviation a few years before at the airport in Montevideo, Uruguay, and he was impressed that I had flown the Cessna 170 from New York to Argentina. When we met again in Paraguay, he immediately gave me a commercial license so I could do private bush and charter flying for hire.

I also made friends with another pilot, Bob Eaton. He was a North American rancher who owned a Cessna 180, a great bush plane, and he had a contract to fly support for a U.S. road-building company and also a U.S. oil-drilling company. Both companies were working in the same area of the Paraguayan Chaco, the northwest area of the country that is only partly civilized with cattle ranches; the rest is a mixture of jungle, mesquite thorny brush, and some clearings with wild grass. A large river runs through Paraguay from north to south, dividing the country into two almost equal halves.

These two U.S. companies, both with English-speaking employees, were working in the same northwest half. They needed an English-speaking pilot. The construction company was improving 150 miles of an existing dirt road and they had already added 150 miles of a new dirt road, way past the cattle ranches and up into uninhabited brush and low jungle. They were now about three hundred miles from Asunción. The oil-drilling company was drilling test wells in the same remote area where the road had reached. My friend flew one to three people and occasional small or light spare parts for equipment maintenance back and forth from Asunción to the site of the two crews.

That Saturday morning, totally out of the blue, Bob called and asked me to do him a favor. He had a conflict and could not fly that day, and his backup pilot was off on another trip. Could I fly his Cessna 180 for him? All I needed to do was fly three people out for one company and bring two or three back to Asunción for the other company. Bob's plane was fueled and checked, and passengers were waiting at the airport. The key was in the plane.

Fun! I was delighted. I was ready and could get to the hangar in fifteen minutes. Bob trusted me to fly it without a checkout or instructions, and I needed no experience navigating because I would just follow the new road out, unload and reload passengers, and fly back down the road to the city. It was a no-brainer.

The road-building company was pushing their road through the flat country at a direction of 315 degrees, clearing about a mile or two a day, adding dirt to raise the roadbed above the surrounding level and packing it into a hard, all-weather surface. They would also make a new airstrip alongside the road about every twenty miles. All I had to do was fly the road guys out to the last airstrip about three hundred miles, or two hours at the normal slow cruise of a Cessna 180. (A new model would fly at 160–170 mph but Bob flew his older plane at about 150.) The oil company would bring their passengers to the same airstrip and I would then fly back down the road to Asunción.

I did a walk around the plane. It was really old and looked worn out, but Bob told me it had a new engine and big tanks, so that meant seven hours of fuel on board. I climbed a ladder at the front of the wing and stuck my finger into the fuel tank—it was full to the brim. I moved over to the tank on the other wing and found it also was full. I checked the oil and the fuel sump drain for water or dirt. Both were okay. I walked around the plane checking the control hinges, the tail wheel, the pitot tube, etc. We loaded up and I cranked the engine and rolled out to take off.

The owner had told me the radio was not working, so the tower, which knew the plane, gave me a green light to taxi to the active runway. I tested the engine and prop and magnetos and carb heat and mixture control. All engine instruments were in the green. The engine sounded great, the brakes were solid, the controls free, and the tower gave me another green light. We took off.

We climbed northward and turned west to cross the big river that came down from Mato Grosso, a state in Brazil. I was going to take a course of 315 degrees when the passenger in the copilot seat, who worked for the road-building company, pointed out where their road began. He was proud of what they had accomplished. He said they had created new records in fast road-building and outstanding quality. He explained that the first 150 miles went from the river to a small religious Mennonite community. It was a pre-existing road out into the cattle-raising country and that small town. They had put in another 150 miles of totally new road to an outpost of the 1930s war with Bolivia, which Paraguay had won. Now they were at kilometer post 480 (300 miles), which I already knew. My passenger was talkative and had lots of information about the ranches we were passing, their airstrips, etc., all of which interested me greatly.

My passenger also pointed out that some airstrips had green grass and some had dirt or very little grass. He said it indicated the different kinds of soils and their relative ability to retain moisture year-round for pasture for cattle. He explained that one ranch of a hundred thousand acres might be able to carry twice the number of cattle as a neighboring ranch if its soil was richer. To a banker, that was important information. In Argentina and Uruguay, the soils were much more uniform and the rainfall much more dependable. Here in the Paraguayan Chaco, moisture control was a big issue.

Another interesting feature my passenger wanted to tell me was that the Chaco ranchers drove their cattle over land to market in Asunción, just like cowboys in the U.S. had done a hundred years before. My passenger also told me that the ranchers did not move their cattle in a straight line down the road to market. The road crossed many small rivers and thus had bridges. They were not made for cattle drives. The rivers were full of flesh-eating piranha fish, so the ranchers drove their cattle over to the Paraguay River, where cattle boats could take their herds downstream to the packing plants without crossing the rivers.* If they did cross a river, they had to sacrifice a few head of cattle by killing them either upstream or downstream to draw the piranha away from the crossing when they had cattle in the water.

The flight was interesting because of my well-informed passenger. At the two-hour mark we saw our destination dirt strip. I landed amid a cloud of dust; newly made dirt strips are always dusty. A pickup was waiting for my passengers, and we said goodbye. I looked for my next passengers, but they were not there. An hour went by, then another. The afternoon was wasting away, and I was a little impatient.

---

* Paraguay only had three large meatpacking plants—slaughterhouses and canning facilities for producing canned corned beef, mostly for Europe. They had no facilities for frozen meat for export.

Finally, a pickup arrived in a cloud of dust and the driver told me that the oil-well people had been held up by a drilling crisis but they would be along shortly. The problem had to do with the samples coming up from the drill head several thousand feet down below the surface. Each drill site had been chosen by the company archeologist, and each one was a different oil-bearing structure, meaning that they were "wildcat" wells. The driver said that the samples coming up from the well would determine if they would drill more or stop right where they were.

It was sundown when the truck arrived again. Two big problems, the driver said. One was that they had to get back to Asunción that night in order to take information back to their head office on the early-morning Braniff flight to the States. The other was news from Asunción that a front was moving in and that it was raining in the city. I had already noticed that the sky was clouding over, another reason I was anxious to get going. We were in a dry area and Asunción was at the edge of the area with frequent tropical rainstorms. The good news was that this front had no lightning and no thunderstorms.

My passengers arrived but it was now dark and I was a bit uneasy. The plane had a great engine and prop, but it was for VFR flying only. It had no radio, no direction finder, and no gyro instruments for blind flying. It did have one old-fashioned gyro, a turn-and-bank instrument driven by suction, not from an engine-driven vacuum pump but by a venturi tube out in the slipstream, which worked when the speed of the airplane was over 80 mph. I told the passengers of the risks, but they were really anxious to catch their plane in the morning and wanted to head back.

During my Navy flight training, we had done some practicing in partial-panel instrument flying. That is, flying under a hood with the main gyros covered—no directional gyro and no artificial horizon to fly by. The magnetic compass was your directional control and the altimeter kept you from running into the ground. Of course, you cannot see the ground at night, and in the Chaco there was not a single electric light bulb for three hundred miles, until you hit the outskirts of Asunción. It meant two hours flying blind, relying only on the magnetic compass to steer by and the altimeter so I wouldn't fly into the ground. I felt we would be fine because there was no hill, smokestack, high-tension line, or even a telephone line in the whole three hundred miles.

I trusted the instruments to keep me flying flat as a billiard table at a safe altitude. I trusted the compass and the engine. The big problem with flying above the clouds or in the clouds is getting back down so you can see the ground or the landing field. We would not get into the clouds at all. The rain was not too heavy from what they were saying, so even though I was not going to see forward through a rainy windshield, I could look down safely to see if there were electric lights under me. Remember, Lindbergh flew from New York to Paris without any gyros except a venturi-driven turn-and-bank indicator, and without seeing forward through a windscreen. He sat in the back behind his gas tanks and just looked down or out to the side.

We loaded up and took off. A pickup truck at the far end of the strip pointed his lights at us and we took off. The plane had functioning instrument lights. I had been told that the weather pattern for the Chaco was always a ceiling of about two thousand feet above the terrain below, which is flyable. We were in total darkness; there were no lights except for kerosene lamps in the Chaco. The venturi came awake shortly after takeoff, so we did have the turn-and-bank. I turned slowly as we climbed and took up a course of exactly 135 degrees to fly back down the invisible road underneath us. I checked my math: 315 degrees northwest going out and 180 degrees less to return was 135 for magnetic course to return. I nailed that. Altitude was three thousand feet above sea level, which was one thousand feet above the ground, and I nailed that. All I had to do was hold the course and hold the altitude, and in two hours we would see lights under us and I could find the airport with its very powerful rotating beacon.

The rain started hitting us half an hour after takeoff. The storm front was moving faster than expected. My Navy training was a blessing, and I was really grateful for it that night. I missed having a full panel of gyros and a radio direction finder, but we were OK, I thought.

Then it happened. One hour and thirty minutes after takeoff, I saw electric lights underneath me. Not bright, but no denying it—we were over a town with lights. Impossible! It was forty-five minutes too soon. Good heavens, I thought. I've gotten us lost. Not just a little bit, but really lost. Could I have flown east into Brazil? No, I couldn't have been that far off. Could I have flown north into Bolivia? Not a chance. Could I have flown south into Argentina? That's exactly what I had done.

If I had flown due south, 180 degrees on the compass, then in one hour and thirty minutes I had to be 225 miles across the border and into Argentina. On the Argentine Chaco side there was a railroad going from the Paraná River to Jujuy at the base of the Andes mountains. There would be towns on the railroad that would have electricity. I had to make a timed instrument turn in order to rotate exactly 90 degrees toward Asunción. When I looked down and saw lights, I saw that we were not only flying in the rain but we were also flying in and out of wispy clouds.

I lowered our altitude five hundred feet to be under the clouds. I did a timed turn, because a magnetic compass does not turn exactly like it should. I knew that the turn-and-bank instrument is two needle widths for three degrees' turn per second. To turn to the left would take thirty seconds for 90 degrees to produce a new heading of 90 degrees, or due east.

Then I had to figure out what was wrong with the magnetic compass in the plane. Before any instrument flight, a pilot has to check the magnetic compass to see if it agrees with the runway heading. Also, a good pilot sets his directional gyro to agree with the compass heading and the runway heading and you recheck it thirty seconds and then one minute after takeoff to see how much it is drifting or processing off the exact runway heading. Then you can trust your directional gyro. I had done none of that, but I expected no night flight or rain, and I thought I had a good compass.

My mental calculations also had to refigure the visible compass number. If flying at 135 degrees southeast produced a ground track of 180 degrees, or due south, I needed to make a 90-degree turn to the left, which would create a direct new course to Asunción of 90 degrees, or true east. I did my thirty-second right-angle timed turn to the left and took up a new course of 045. I explained to my passengers that a bad compass had led us off course, but we would see lights under us in about eighty minutes.

I breathed a sigh of relief when at one hour and twenty minutes, we saw lights under us. A few more minutes and we saw the big river under us, and soon we could see the rotating beacon of the airport tower.

We landed and unloaded, getting a little wet but safe and sound after two and a half hours of blind flying on a rainy night.

I offered multiple thanks to my Heavenly Father for His help and promised to never again get caught flying blind in a rainstorm with no gyros, no radios, and a bad compass.

I called my friend who had trusted me with his old plane. I told him about flying back in the rain with no instruments, and asked if he was aware that his compass was off by at least 45 degrees.

"Oh yeah," Bob said. "I guess I forgot to tell you about that!"

Story Four

VISIT TO A SUGAR MILL

W E HAD A good client who owned a big sugar mill in the town of Villarrica, about a hundred miles east of Asunción. The bank had made a loan that was secured with bags of sugar in their warehouse, so we had to make a physical survey of the collateral before our inspectors performed their next surprise audit. Time went by and suddenly a junior credit officer reminded me that if we did not go out to Villarrica and perform that inspection, we would be in big trouble with our own bank auditors.

No one had the time to go because it would take several hours by car on bad roads each way. A whole day would be lost. I decided I could fly my plane half an hour to the mill, land on their grass strip, walk to the warehouse, get it done, fly home, and be back at the bank well before noon.

I phoned the Asunción office of the sugar company and told them my plan. All I needed was the key to the warehouse. The manager said he would drive out the day before I arrived to ensure that everything was in order.

Then he added, "Señor Wells, have you been to the mill and the warehouse before?"

"No, not really," I answered. "I thought the airstrip was right beside the warehouse. Isn't it?"

He clarified the layout for me. "The grass strip is next to the mill. Next comes a large holding area for ox teams and tractors pulling loaded wagons with freshly cut sugarcane to the refinery mill, and then on the far side is the warehouse along a railroad spur for freight cars. It is actually a bit of a walk in the hot sun. There is no path nor road."

He paused for a few seconds and then said, "I understand you are comfortable on a horse. Why don't I meet you with a saddlehorse when you land? We can ride over to the warehouse together."

I thought it was a great idea.

"I'll be flying the low-wing Bonanza with retractable gear," I told the manager. "Is the grass mowed? Grass that's too high gets clogged in the wheels."

He assured me the grass would be mowed.

I flew the plane over to Villarrica the next day. As I descended, I could see the manager waiting on his horse and a second man on horseback holding the reins of a third horse. They were behind a fence. I landed, taxied over, and shut the engine down. They opened a gate and rode toward me while I got out of the plane and waited in front of the wing.

As they got closer, suddenly the manager shouted in alarm, pointing at the grass in front of the three horses and at my feet, and shouted, "Snake! Jump! Jump on your wing! It's poisonous!"

He sounded frightened, and that startled me. They said I did an impossible vertical jump at least three feet up in the air as if someone had lit a rocket under me. I landed on the wing. The bright green snake zipped through the newly mowed grass between my legs, or at least between my boot prints where I had been standing. The three horses had frightened the snake and it sped toward where my legs had been planted.

The manager, still agitated, exclaimed, "That is a very dangerous snake. It is so poisonous that it is called 'una víbora de cinco minutos!' If he bites you, you have only five minutes to live. There is no known antidote."

I got off the wing and was relieved when I was finally in the saddle. At the warehouse, I counted the ten thousand bags of refined sugar ready for export. Then we rode back, and I moved my horse as close to the plane as I could get. I put one boot on the grass and the other foot onto the metal step of the plane, then climbed onto the wing and into the cabin. I was back in the bank before 11:00 a.m. and had a good story to tell the kids that night.

Story Five

A NOISY FLYING MONSTER

ONE DAY IN Asunción, my pilot friend Bob Eaton
returned from the Chaco with a really wild story.

The road crew had been leading the way with the first
bulldozer, digging the brush and trees out of what would be the
roadbed. No one had seen any Nivacle* indigenous people in the
area, but the tractor driver had seen an arrow or two fly by without
hitting anything. He had screens for protection so plowed ahead.

---

* Formerly known as the Chulupi, the Nivacle people have lived for thousands
of years in the region between Bolivia and Brazil.

Bob landed his Cessna 180 at the very last airstrip but had some time on his hands until the next passengers arrived for the return trip. He made his way over to an airconditioned trailer parked a few blocks away through the brush and waited there. When his passengers arrived, they rode back to the Cessna in a pickup truck. When they came within sight of the plane, they all gasped.

What a disaster! The Nivacle tribe had attacked the plane, apparently thinking it was some kind of noisy flying monster. They wanted to kill the "bird." Their arrows did not faze the aluminum skin, so they had attacked the insides of it. They used their knives to tear out the seats and the headliner. They were mystified by the plexiglass and did not bother it. They hammered at the panel and did some damage.

Bob found a wooden box to sit on, and his passengers just sat on the floor of the plane. It was a two-hour trip back. From then on, the companies provided armed protection for their crews, pilots, and aircraft.

ABOUT THE AUTHOR

ROBERT E. WELLS, a native of Nevada, is a former executive for Citibank and emeritus General Authority of The Church of Jesus Christ of Latter-day Saints. After serving in the U.S. Navy in World War II, he graduated in accounting and economics from Brigham Young University, then served a mission for the Church in Argentina. He married the former Meryl Leavitt in 1952 and directed Citibank operations in Argentina, Uruguay, Brazil, Paraguay, and Ecuador. He and his family later lived in Mexico, Chile, and Guatemala, where he supervised some two million missionaries and Church members. After Meryl passed away in 1960, he married the former Helen Walser in 1962. They have a blended family of seven children, along with twenty-seven grandchildren and thirty-eight great-grandchildren. At age 93, he still lives by his motto: "I love the spirit of adventure and adventures of the spirit!"